IMPROVING YOUR WRITTEN ENGLISH

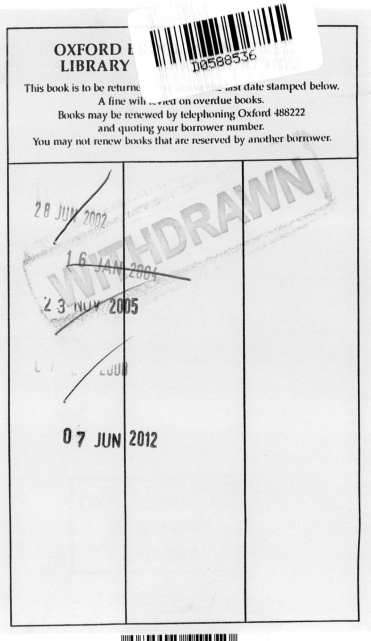

GENERAL REFERENCE

IMPROVING YOUR WRITTEN ENGLISH

How to sharpen up your grammar,
punctuation and spelling for everyday use

Marion Field

2nd edition

How To Books

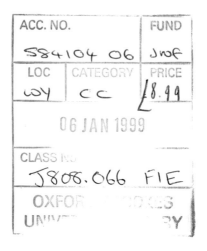
Cartoons by Mike Flanagan

British Library Cataloguing-in-Publication data
A catalogue record for this book is available from the British Library.

First published by How To Books Ltd, 3 Newtec Place,
Magdalen Road, Oxford OX4 1RE, United Kingdom.
Tel: (01865) 793806. Fax: (01865) 248780.

First edition 1997
Second edition 1998

Note: The material contained in this book is set out in good faith for
general guidance and no liability can be accepted for loss or expense
incurred as a result of relying in particular circumstances on statements
made in the book. The laws and regulations are complex and liable to
change, and readers should check the current position with the relevant
authorities before making personal arrangements.

Produced for How To Books by Deer Park Productions.
Typeset by Kestrel Data, Exeter.
Printed and bound in Great Britain by Cromwell Press,
Trowbridge, Wiltshire.

Contents

List of illustrations   8

Preface   9

PART ONE: THE BASICS

1 Punctuation   11

Knowing when to stop   11
Using commas correctly   13
Making use of the semi-colon, colon and dash   16
Remembering the question mark and the exclamation mark   18
Checklist   19
Practising what you've learnt   19
Discussion points   20

2 Grammar   21

Making sense of your sentence   21
Using words correctly   26
Linking ideas together   29
Colouring your writing   33
Using prepositions   35
Paragraphing your work   36
Setting out direct speech   38
Checklist   42
Practising what you've learnt   43
Discussion points   45

3 Spelling   46

Establishing the ground rules   46
Avoiding common mistakes   49
Using a dictionary   51

Making use of the thesaurus   52
Checklist   53
Practising what you've learnt   53
Discussion points   54

4   Apostrophes and abbreviations   55

Using apostrophes to show possession   55
Abbreviating words   57
Handling contractions   58
Using acronyms   59
Checklist   59
Practising what you've learnt   60
Discussion points   60

5   Correct English   61

Recognising common mistakes   61
Avoiding unnecessary repetition   66
Making comparisons   67
Eliminating jargon   69
Stimulating your imagination   70
Improving your style   72
Checklist   76
Practising what you've learnt   76
Discussion points   77

PART TWO: ENGLISH IN ACTION

6   Writing an essay and a short story   78

Researching your essay   78
Making notes   79
Planning your work   80
Structuring your essay   80
Writing your essay   82
Plotting a short story   83
Checking your work   84
Checklist   84
Practising what you've learnt   85
Discussion points   85

7   Summarising and reporting   86

Producing a readable summary   86

Compiling a report   87
Checklist   89
Practising what you've learnt   91
Discussion points   91

8 Filling in forms   **92**

Providing the basic information   92
Understanding what is required   92
Writing legibly   101
Asking for help   101
Reading the forms   102
Signing your name   102
Checklist   102
Practising what you've learnt   102
Discussion points   103

9 Writing letters   **104**

Writing a personal letter   104
Writing a formal letter   106
Planning your letter   107
Finishing your letter   109
Writing different types of letters   109
Checklist   114
Practising what you've learnt   114
Discussion points   115

10 Applying for a job   **116**

Preparing a Curriculum Vitae   116
Filling in an application form   121
Writing a covering letter   122
Including references   122
Checklist   124
Practising what you've learnt   124
Discussion points   125

Suggested Answers   126

Glossary   131

Further Reading   133

Index   134

List of Illustrations

1. Would you like to be able to . . .   12
2. Commonly misspelled words   50
3. Essay plan   81
4. Title page of report   88
5. Introduction to report   88
6. Summary of report   89
7. Recommendations from report   90
8. Example of market research form   93
9. Personal details on any form   93
10. Form for opening a bank account   94
11. Form for opening a mortgage account   95
12. Standing order form   96
13. Patient registration form   97
14. Application for a department charge card   98
15. Department store wedding gift list   98
16. Car insurance form   99
17. Handwritten personal letter   105
18. Formal letter   108
19. Addressed envelope   109
20. Handwritten letter of sympathy   110
21. Letter requesting a photograph   111
22. Handwritten letter to a local newspaper   112
23. Letter of complaint   113
24. CV: personal details   116
25. CV: career history   119
26. Example of a CV   120
27. Application form   121
28. Covering letter   123

Preface
to the Second Edition

Do you have trouble with punctuation? Are you always using commas instead of full stops? Is your spelling weak? Do you have difficulty filling in forms and writing letters? Then this book will help you improve the standard of your written English. It has been written in an easy-to-understand way designed for use by anyone. Whether you are a student, school-leaver, an employed or self-employed worker or someone at home, it should prove a valuable reference book.

The format is easy to follow with plenty of examples. At the end of each section there is an opportunity to practise what you have learnt. Suggested answers are at the back of the book.

Part 1 deals with the basic rules of punctuation identifying the various punctuation marks and showing how each is used. It also covers the parts of speech and demonstrates their uses. Part 2 shows you how to put Part 1 into practice. There are sections on essay writing, summarising, writing reports and even plotting a short story. There are also chapters on letter writing, filling in forms and applying for a job.

Written in a simple style with frequent headings and easily identifiable revision points, this book should prove invaluable for anyone who needs help in improving his or her written English for whatever reason.

Marion Field

Is This You?

School-leaver

GCSE student

Foreign student

Aspiring writer

A-level student

Mature student

Secretary

Housewife

University student

Job-seeker

Teacher

Typist

Self-employed

Hotelier

College-leaver

Office temp

Office junior

Retired

Computer programmer

Receptionist

Returner to work

Mailing clerk

Hairdresser

Sales assistant

Home worker

Personal secretary

Office worker

Unemployed

Common entrance student

Writer

Social worker

Personnel manager

Private tutor

Tour guide

Lecturer

Sales clerk

Police officer

Marketing assistant

Travel agent

Nurse

Bookshop assistant

Businessperson

Actor

Foreign businessperson

Retailer

Legal secretary

Youth leader

Window dresser

Departmental manager

Part One: The Basics
1
Punctuation

KNOWING WHEN TO STOP

Writing it wrongly

My name is Marion Field I'm a freelance writer and I write articles for various magazines I live near several motorways so I can easily drive around the country to do my research the airport is also near me I love travelling and I've visited many different parts of the world this gives me the opportunity to write travel articles I enjoy taking photographs.

Have you run out of breath yet? I'm sure you soon would if you were given no opportunity to stop.

> Without full stops, writing would make little sense.

Writing it correctly
Let's try again.

My name is Marion Field. I'm a freelance writer and I write articles for various magazines. I live near several motorways so I can easily drive around the country to do my research. The airport is also near me. I love travelling and I've visited many different parts of the world. This gives me the opportunity to write travel articles. I enjoy taking photographs.

That's better, isn't it? Because it is now broken up into sentences, it makes sense. Each statement is complete in itself and the full stop separates it from the next one.

WOULD YOU LIKE TO BE ABLE TO

1. Improve your writing skills? _____
2. Avoid grammatical errors? _____
3. Increase your accuracy? _____
4. Widen your vocabulary? _____
5. Improve your spelling? _____
6. Use punctuation correctly? _____
7. Improve your sentence structure? _____
8. Use apostrophes correctly? _____
9. Avoid common spelling errors? _____
10. Improve the quality of your writing? _____
11. Avoid misusing words? _____
12. Produce well-structured pieces of writing? _____
13. Re-draft your work effectively? _____
14. Correct your work effectively? _____
15. Write more convincingly? _____
16. Develop your writing style? _____
17. Write in a variety of forms? _____
18. Present your work more attractively? _____
19. Increase your potential? _____
20. Write more fluently? _____
21. Sharpen your writing? _____
22. Write a concise report? _____
23. Produce a well-rounded essay? _____
24. Complete a satisfactory assignment? _____
25. Write an interesting letter? _____
26. Write a short story? _____
27. Produce convincing dialogue? _____
28. Create a vivid description? _____
29. Produce sparkling prose? _____
30. Increase your word power? _____
31. Write a competent letter of application? _____
32. Fill in a complicated form? _____
33. Produce a well-presented CV? _____
34. Write a business letter? _____
35. Communicate more effectively? _____
36. Increase your awareness of the uses of language? _____
37. Organise your writing more carefully? _____
38. Plan your assignments more effectively? _____

Fig. 1. Would you like to be able to . . .

Commas can't replace full stops

Beware of using **commas** instead of **full stops**.

What is wrong with this piece?

She entered the library, it was crowded with people, she didn't know any of them and she wished she'd stayed at home, she felt so lonely.

Did you find the mistakes? Here is the corrected version:

She entered the library. It was crowded with people. She didn't know any of them and she wished she'd stayed at home. She felt so lonely.

The use of **commas** will be explained in the next section. They have a particular role to play but they can _never_ take the place of **full stops**. Full stops are used to separate sentences, each of which should make complete sense on its own. Each one must be constructed properly and end with a full stop. There will be more about sentence structure in the next chapter.

Revising the points
● A full stop should be used to separate statements that are complete in themselves.

● Commas should never be used instead of full stops.

● Full stops make sense of your writing.

USING COMMAS CORRECTLY

Breaking up a list
We have already noted the incorrect use of **commas** in the previous section. Now let's look at how they should be used.

Use **commas** to separate the items in a list. In this case the last one must be preceded by 'and':

Johnny played hockey, soccer, rugby, lacrosse _and_ tennis.

(*not*: Johnny played hockey, soccer, rugby, lacrosse, tennis.)

> Kit was listening to her Walkman, David was trying to do his homework, Mum was getting the supper ready and Dad was reading the paper.

If the 'and' had been missed out and a comma used instead after 'ready', it would have been wrong. Here is the incorrect version:

> Kit was listening to her Walkman, David was trying to do his homework, Mum was getting the supper ready, Dad was reading the paper.

Look at the following example. Is it right or wrong?

> The sea was calm, the sun was shining, the beach was empty, Anne felt at peace with the world.

Of course it's wrong. The comma after 'empty' should be removed and 'and' inserted instead:

> The sea was calm, the sun was shining, the beach was empty and Anne felt at peace with the world.

Beginning a sentence with a conjunction (joining word)

If you begin a sentence with a **conjunction** (joining word), put a **comma** to separate the first part of the sentence from the rest of it. In the sentence I've just written 'if' is a conjunction and there is a comma after 'word'. There will be more about conjunctions in the next chapter.

Here are two more examples with the conjunctions underlined. Notice where the comma is placed:

> Because it was raining, we stayed inside.

> As the sun set, the sky glowed red.

Separating groups of words by commas

Commas are also used to separate groups of words which are in the middle of the main sentence, as in the following sentence:

Clive, who had just changed schools, found it difficult to adjust to his new surroundings.

'Clive' is the subject of the sentence and 'who had just changed schools' says a little more about him so therefore it is enclosed by commas.

If commas are missed out, the sense of the sentence is sometimes lost or it has to be read twice. Sometimes the meaning can be changed by the placing of the comma. Look at the following:

As mentioned first impressions can be misleading.

Where would you place the comma? After 'mentioned'?

As mentioned, first impressions can be misleading.

But it *could* be placed after 'first' and then the meaning is changed:

As mentioned first, impressions can be misleading.

Which do you prefer? Which makes more sense?

Using commas before a question
Here is another example of the use of a **comma**:

I don't like her dress, do you?

A comma is always used before expressions like 'do you?', 'don't you?', 'isn't it?', 'won't you?' These are usually used in dialogue (speech). There will be more about this in the next chapter.

Example
'You will come to the play, won't you?'

'I'd love to. It's by Alan Ayckbourn, isn't it?'

Using commas before a name
A **comma** should also be used when addressing a person by name. This would also be used in dialogue:

'Do be quiet, Sarah.'

'John, where are you?'

Using commas in direct speech

Always use a **comma** to separate direct speech from the rest of the sentence unless a question mark or an exclamation mark has been used. There will be more about these and the setting out of dialogue in the next chapter.

Example

He pleaded, 'Let's go to MacDonalds.'

'I can't,' she replied.

Revising the points

● Use commas to separate words and groups of words in a list.

● Use a comma if you begin a sentence with a conjunction or to separate groups of words within the main sentence.

● Use a comma before expressions like 'isn't it?' and also when addressing someone by name.

● Use a comma to separate direct speech from the rest of the sentence.

MAKING USE OF THE SEMI-COLON, COLON AND DASH

Using the semi-colon

The **semi-colon** is a useful punctuation mark although it is not used a great deal. It can be used when you don't feel you need a full stop; usually the second statement follows closely on to the first one. Don't use a capital letter after a semi-colon.

Example

It was growing very dark; there was obviously a storm brewing.

The idea of 'a storm' follows closely the 'growing very dark'. A full stop is not necessary but don't be tempted to use a comma.

- A comma can never be used to separate two statements.

- A semi-colon can be used to separate groups of statements which follow naturally on from one another:

    The storm clouds gathered; the rain started to fall; the thunder rolled; the lightning flashed.

A semi-colon can also help to emphasise a statement:

    The thieves had done a good job; every drawer and cupboard had been ransacked.

The strength of the second statement would have been weakened if a conjunction had been used instead of a semi-colon. Look at the altered sentence:

    The thieves had done a good job because every drawer and cupboard had been ransacked.

A semi-colon can also be used when you wish to emphasise a contrast as in the following sentence:

    Kate may go to the disco; you may not.

'You may not' stands out starkly because it stands alone.

Using the colon
A **colon** can be used for two purposes. It can introduce a list of statements as in the following sentence:

    There are three good reasons why you got lost: you had no map, it was dark and you have no sense of direction.

Like the **semi-colon,** you need no capital letter after it. It can also be used to show two statements reinforcing each other:

    Your punctuation is weak: you must learn when to use full stops.

Using the dash

A **dash** is used for emphasis. What is said between dashes – or after the dash if there is only one – is more emphatic than if there were no dash. If you break your sentence in the middle to make an added point, use a dash before and after it:

> Janice, Elaine, Maureen, Elsie – in fact all the girls – can go on the trip to London.

If the added section is at the end of the sentence, only one dash is needed:

> This is the second time you have not done your English homework – or any of your homework.

REMEMBERING THE QUESTION MARK AND THE EXCLAMATION MARK

Using the question mark

The **question mark** is obviously placed at the end of a question. *Do* remember to put it there. From my experience as a teacher, I've found that students frequently miss it out through carelessness.

Example

> Is it raining?

> You won't go out in the rain, will you?

If you are using direct speech, the question mark takes the place of the comma and is always placed inside the inverted commas (speech marks):

> 'When is your interview?' asked Lucy.

> 'Are you travelling by train?' queried John.

Using the exclamation mark

The **exclamation mark** should be used rarely or it loses its impact. It should not be used for emphasis; your choice of words should be sufficient. It is used in direct speech – again in place of a comma – when the speaker is exclaiming. There should always be an exclamation mark if the word 'exclaimed' is used:

> 'I don't believe it!' he exclaimed.

However, the word 'exclaimed' is not always necessary. It can merely be suggested:

> 'I can't reach it!' she cried.

In this example a comma could have been used but an exclamation mark is more appropriate.

The only other place where an exclamation mark can be used is where there is an element of irony in the statement. The speaker or writer comments with 'tongue in cheek'. What is said is not literally true but is said to make a point:

> Jean's Christmas card arrived a year late. It had been on a trip round the world!

CHECKLIST

● When do you use a **full stop**?

● List five uses of the **comma**.

● When should you use a **semi-colon** and a **colon**?

● What use does the **dash** have?

● When do you use a **question mark** and an **exclamation mark**?

PRACTISING WHAT YOU'VE LEARNT

Punctuate the following extracts:

1. John was furious he stormed out of the house slamming the door behind him never again would he try to help anyone he'd gone to see Peter to offer financial aid and Peter had angrily thrown his offer back in his face surely he could have shown

some gratitude now he would be late for work and he had an early appointment with an important client

2. The sun shone down from a brilliant blue sky the slight breeze ruffled the long grass the scent of roses was all around and the birds were twittering happily in the trees Emma who had been feeling sad suddenly felt more cheerful the summer had come at last hadn't it while she wandered down the garden path she thought about the letter she'd received that morning.

3. The team those who were present lined up to meet the new manager they had had a bad season Clive hoped Brian would improve their chance of promotion at the moment the team was a disaster the goalkeeper never saw the ball until it was too late the defence players were too slow and the captain was indecisive.

4. I don't believe it she exclaimed
   Why not he enquired
   Surely it could not be true why hadn't she been told before it wasn't fair why was she always the last to hear anything if she'd been the one going to New York she'd probably only have heard about it after she should have left why had Pat been offered the chance of a lifetime hadn't she worked just as hard.

See page 126 for suggested answers.

DISCUSSION POINTS

1. What is the purpose of punctuation?

2. Why do you need several different punctuation marks?

3. What purpose does each serve?

2
Grammar

MAKING SENSE OF YOUR SENTENCE

Using nouns correctly
Office, letters, boss, desk, computer, clock.

I'm sure you'd agree that the above is *not* a sentence. Can you explain why?

It is only a list of 'things' which are called **nouns**. But each of the above words can be the 'subject' of the sentence if it is linked to a **verb**:

The office <u>was</u> closed.

The letters <u>arrived</u> late.

The boss <u>had</u> lunch early.

Her desk <u>collapsed</u>.

His computer <u>crashed.</u>

The clock <u>was</u> slow.

Each of the underlined words is a **verb**.

> A **noun**, the 'subject' of the sentence, must be linked to a **verb** if it is to make sense.

Using verbs correctly
A **verb** is a 'doing' or 'being' word.

> There must be at least one **verb** in a sentence or it is not a
> sentence.

Understanding verbs

Verbs can be either **finite** or **non-finite**.

Finite verbs

Finite verbs must show **tense**. They can be past, present or future
and are always connected to a noun or a **pronoun**. (There is more
about pronouns in the next section.)

In the following examples, which are the verbs and which tenses
are being used?

> Tomorrow I will go to London.
>
> Yesterday she was very unhappy.
>
> He plays the piano very well.

I'm sure you knew the answers.

> 'will go' is the future tense.
>
> 'was' is the past tense.
>
> 'plays' is the present tense.

Non-finite verbs

The non-finite verbs are the infinitive form of the verb and the
present and past participles.

The inifinitive

The **infinitive** is the form of the verb that has 'to' before it:

> To run, to dance, to write, to publish, to dine.

Many people consider it incorrect to use a 'split infinitive'. This is
when a word is placed between the 'to' and the verb:

> It is difficult <u>to</u> accurately <u>assess</u> the data.

The following example is better. The infinitive 'to assess' has not been 'split' by the adverb 'accurately':

It is difficult accurately <u>to assess</u> the data.

Past participles

The **past participle** is used with the verb 'to have'; it then forms a finite verb. Either the present or the past tense of the verb 'to have' can be used. It will depend on the context. Look at the following examples. The past participles are underlined:

She had <u>scratched</u> her arm.

He has <u>passed</u> his examination.

Joan has <u>cooked</u> the dinner.

Colin had <u>written</u> a letter to his mother.

The first three past participles in the examples above are the same as the ordinary past tense but 'has' or 'had' have been added. In the last example the past participle 'written' is different and can only be used with the verb 'to have'.

Present participles

The **present participle** always ends in '-ing' and is introduced by the verb 'to be'. The past or present tense of the verb 'to be' can be used:

Ian is <u>helping</u> his mother.

Julie was <u>doing</u> her homework.

Using the gerund

The present participle can also be used as a **noun** and in this case it is called a **gerund**:

<u>Shopping</u> is fun.

The <u>wailing</u> was continuous

Using the present participle as an adjective

Certain present participles can also be used as adjectives:

The <u>crying</u> child ran to its mother.

The <u>howling</u> dog kept the family awake.

Now look at the following examples.

Rushed across the road.

Came into the shop.

Are these sentences? No, of course they aren't. Although they each have a **verb**, they have no 'subject' linked to them. We don't know *who* rushed across the road or came into the shop. Add a **noun** and it makes sense:

The <u>cat</u> rushed across the road.

<u>Laura</u> came into the shop.

'Laura' is a **proper noun** as it is the name of a person. Names always, of course, start with capital letters. Other nouns are known as **common nouns**.

In each sentence there must be a **noun** which is linked to a **verb**.

Replacing nouns with pronouns

<u>It</u> rushed across the road.

<u>She</u> came into the shop.

'It' replaces 'the cat' and 'she' replaces 'Laura'. Both are **pronouns** and take the place of a **noun**. **Personal pronouns** are identified as 1st, 2nd and 3rd **persons**. Look at the following table:

	Singular	*Plural*
1st person	I	We
2nd person	You	You
3rd person	He, she, it	They

Notice that the 2nd person is the same in both the singular and plural. In the past 'thou' was used as the singular but today 'you' is in general use for both, although 'thou' may be heard occasionally in some parts of the country.

> The 'subject' of the sentence can be either a **common noun** (a thing), a **proper noun** (a name) or a **pronoun** which takes the place of a **noun**.

Using personal pronouns

> I was born in Yorkshire but spent most of my teenage years in Sussex.

Which 'person' is used in this sentence?

The **1st** 'person' is used because the writer is telling his own story. An author writes an 'autobiography' when he writes about his own life.

Look at the following sentence:

> Ellen Terry was born in 1847 and became a very famous actress. She acted in many of Shakespeare's plays.

This is written in the **3rd** person. Someone else is writing about Ellen Terry. She is not telling her own story so the **personal pronoun** used in the second sentence is 'she'. A book written about Ellen Terry by someone else is called a 'biography'.

What about novels?

Novels (books that are fiction although sometimes based on fact) can be written in either the 1st person where the main character is telling the story, or the 3rd person where the author tells a story about a set of characters.

Are books ever written in the 2nd person?

Yes they are. Look at the following example:

> Take two chicken breasts and, using a little fat, brown them in the frying pan, turning them frequently. Mix the sauce

in a saucepan and gently heat it through. When it simmers, pour it over the chicken.

The 'you' in the recipe is 'understood'. 'You' (the **2nd person**) are being told what to do. All instruction books, therefore, are written in the 2nd person.

Revising the points

- Each sentence must contain at least one verb.

- The verb must be linked to the noun which is the subject of the sentence.

- The past participle can be connected to the verb 'to have'.

- The present participle can be connected to the verb 'to be'.

- Nouns can be replaced by pronouns.

- An autobiography is written in the 1st person because the author is telling his own story.

- A biography is written in the 3rd person. It is the story of someone's life told by another person.

- A novel can be written in either the 1st or the 3rd person.

- An instruction manual always uses the 'understood' 2nd person as it gives instructions to the reader.

USING WORDS CORRECTLY

Making verbs agree

In the last section we looked at **personal pronouns**. There are a number of other **pronouns** as well. Because some of these are singular and some are plural, the **verb** is often incorrectly used in the plural form with singular **pronouns**. Look at the following examples:

Each of you have been given a pencil.

Each of you has been given a pencil.

Which is correct? The second example is the correct one. 'Each' is a *singular* pronoun and therefore 'has' should be used as it refers to *one* person or thing. Look at the following examples;

She (one person) has a pencil. (Singular)

They (several people) have been given pencils. (Plural)

Some other pronouns which are singular and should always be followed by the singular form of the verbs are: everyone, nobody, anything, something:

Everyone comes to the match.

Nobody likes her.

Anything is better than that.

Something has fallen off the desk.

> Singular pronouns must always agree with the rest of the sentence.

Everyone has their own books.

The above example is incorrect. 'Everyone' is singular. 'Their' and 'books' are plural so 'his' (or 'her') and 'book' should be used. Here is the correct version:

Everyone has his own book.

Using collective nouns correctly

Some nouns are singular but represent a group of people or things. They are called **collective nouns** and, like singular pronouns, must always be followed by the singular form of the verb. Look at the following common mistake:

The Government are preparing a new Divorce Bill.

What is wrong with it? 'Government' is a *singular* noun. There is *one* Government. The correct version is:

> The Government <u>is</u> planning a new Divorce Bill.

Most **collective nouns** can, of course, be made plural by adding an 's'. They are then followed by the plural form of the verb:

> The Governments of France and England are both democratic.

Other collective nouns include team, group, choir, family, class, band. Look at the following examples:

> Our <u>team is</u> top of the league.
>
> That <u>group makes</u> the best cakes.
>
> The school <u>choir has</u> won an award at the Festival.
>
> The <u>family goes</u> to Austria every year.
>
> Her <u>class behaves</u> disgracefully.
>
> His <u>band performs</u> in schools.

Discovering abstract nouns

An abstract noun denotes a 'quality' or 'state'. Some examples are anger, hatred, heat, beauty, honesty, danger and power. Sometimes they can be formed from adjectives by adding the suffix '-ness':

adjectives	*abstract nouns*
sad	sadness
ill	illness
ugly	ugliness
bright	brightness
dark	darkness
kind	kindness

Other abstract nouns are formed differently. Look at the following examples:

adjective	*abstract noun*
high	height
wide	width
patient	patience
wonderful	wonder
pleasant	pleasure

Revising the points

● Singular pronouns must always be followed by singular verbs.

● Collective nouns represent a group of people or things but are singular words.

● Collective nouns must always be followed by singular verbs.

● Abstract nouns denote a quality or state.

LINKING IDEAS TOGETHER

Making use of conjunctions

She was late for work she missed the train

By now you will have learnt that the above sentence is incorrect as there are two **verbs** – 'missed' and 'was' – and no punctuation between the two sections of the sentence. A **full stop** or a **semi-colon** could be placed after train. Here is the correct version:

She missed the train. She was late for work.

or

She missed the train; she was late for work.

However, the example could be made into one sentence by the use of a **conjunction** (joining word). This would make a better sentence:

She missed the train so she was late for work.

or

She was late for work because she missed the train.

Both 'so' and 'because' are **conjunctions** and link together the two sections of the sentence. Other conjunctions are: although, when, if, while, as, before, unless, where, after, since, whether, that.

Linking clauses with conjunctions

Each section of a sentence that contains a subject (**noun**) and a **verb** is called a **clause**. If there is only one in a sentence, it is called a **main clause**. The clauses can be linked together by using **conjunctions** which can be placed between the clauses as in the previous examples. They can also be placed at the beginning of a sentence:

> Because she missed the train, she was late for work.

Notice that there is a **comma** after the first clause. If a sentence starts with a conjunction it *must* be followed by *two* clauses and there should be a comma between them. The clause that is introduced by the conjunction is a **dependent clause** because it 'depends' on the main clause. Look at the following examples:

> Although he had not been successful, he was not discouraged.
>
> *or*
>
> He was not discouraged although he had not been successful.
>
> When her daughter came to stay, she put flowers in the spare room.
>
> *or*
>
> She put flowers in the spare room when her daughter came to stay.

Look at the following:

> This is the coat that I prefer.

When 'that' is used in this way, it can sometimes be omitted without damaging the sentence:

> This is the coat I prefer.

Which do you think sounds better? I believe the second one. It 'tightens' the writing. The 'that' is 'understood' but does not need to be included.

Using 'and' and 'but'

'And' and 'but' are also **conjunctions** but they should not be used to start a sentence. Their place is between **clauses** and they join together **main clauses**:

> I waited for two hours <u>but</u> she did not come.

> He sat at the computer <u>and</u> wrote his article.

- 'And' and 'but' link clauses and should not be used at the beginning of a sentence.

- They can be used at the end of a list of main clauses:

> The radio was on, the baby was banging her spoon on the table, Peter was stamping on the floor <u>and</u> Susan was throwing pieces of paper out of the window.

Each main clause is separated from the next by a comma; 'and' precedes the last clause.

Commas may be used to separate **main clauses** provided the last **clause** is preceded by 'and'.

Joining clauses with relative pronouns

Relative pronouns have a similar function to conjunctions. They link **dependent clauses** to **main clauses**:

> The house, <u>which</u> had once been beautiful, was now a ruin.

'Which' is a **relative pronoun** and, because it and the **dependent clause** both follow the subject of the sentence (the house), it is placed in the middle of the **main clause** and **commas** are used to separate it. The **main clause** is 'The house . . . was now a ruin'. The **dependent clause** is '. . . had once been beautiful . . .'

Other relative pronouns are: who, whose, whom, that.

'That' can be either a **conjunction** or a **relative pronoun**. It depends on how it is used.

Examples

The man, <u>who</u> had been bitten by a dog, became very ill.

The boy, <u>whose</u> bike had been stolen, cried.

The player, <u>whom</u> I supported, lost the match.

Using interrogative pronouns

'Interrogative' implies a question. The same words as the relative pronouns can also be used as **interrogative pronouns** at the start of a question as in the examples below.

Remember that there *must* be a question mark at the end.

<u>Which</u> do you wish to take?

<u>Who</u> is moving into that house?

<u>Whose</u> is that pencil?

Revising the points

● Conjunctions are words that link clauses together.

● If a sentence begins with a conjunction, there must be two clauses following it and they must be separated by a comma.

● Sentences should not start with 'and' or 'but'.

● Relative pronouns are used to introduce a dependent clause in the middle of a main clause.

● Relative pronouns can also introduce a question.

Handling phrases

Do the following words form a sentence?

Leaping off the bus.

No, this is not a sentence. It has no subject connected to it so 'leaping' which is part of a **verb** is not complete. To make it into a sentence we have to add a **noun** and complete the **verb**:

Sheila was leaping off the bus.

It's not a very good sentence, is it? We could use 'leaping off the bus' in another way. Look at the following example:

Leaping off the bus, Sheila rushed across the road.

This makes sense. 'Sheila rushed across the road' is the **main clause** and could stand alone but it has been introduced by 'leaping off the bus' which is a **phrase**.

> A **phrase** is a group of words that does not make sense on its own.

When a phrase starts the sentence, it is followed by a **comma** as in the example above. Phrases add information that is not essential to the sense of the sentence:

Mr Ransome, the retiring Headmaster, made a stirring speech at his farewell dinner.

Mr Ransome is described by the **phrase** 'the retiring Headmaster' but it is not essential for the sense of the sentence.

> **Phrases** add extra information to the sentence.

COLOURING YOUR WRITING

Livening up your writing

You now have the basic 'tools' with which to write a variety of sentences. Some types of writing only require the 'basics'. However, other writing needs to be more colourful. You will need to evoke atmosphere, describe vividly and paint a picture with words.

Utilising adjectives

Adjectives are words that describe **nouns**. They add colour and flesh to your sentence. They must always be related to a noun:

> He bit into the <u>juicy</u> apple.

'Juicy' is an **adjective** which describes the **noun** 'apple'. Isn't it more vivid than the following example?

> He bit into the apple.

If there is a list of adjectives before a noun, separate them with a comma:

> You are the most rude, unkind, objectionable person I have ever met.

If the list of adjectives is at the end of the clause, the last one will be preceded by 'and':

> She was elegant, poised, self-confident and beautiful.

Adjectives are used to enhance **nouns**.

Employing adverbs

Adverbs, as might be expected, **describe** or modify **verbs**. They are often formed by adding '. . . ly' to an **adjective**:

> She dances <u>beautifully.</u>

> He <u>hastily</u> wrote the letter.

Adverbs can also be used to modify or help other adverbs:

> The doctor arrived <u>very</u> promptly.

'Very' is an **adverb** modifying the **adverb** 'promptly'. They can also modify adjectives:

> The patient is <u>much</u> better today.

'Much' is an **adverb** modifying the **adjective** 'better'.

Other adverbs include: too, more and however.

USING PREPOSITIONS

A **preposition** is a word that 'governs' a noun or pronoun and usually comes before it. It indicates the relation of the noun or pronoun to another word. In the following examples the prepositions are underlined. Notice they are all followed by a noun or pronoun.

I knew she was at home.

She ran across the road.

The clouds were massing in the sky.

Her book was under the table.

He told me about it.

There has been a tradition that a preposition should not be placed at the end of a clause or sentence but should always precede the noun or pronoun which it governs:

Who are you talking to?

should therefore be:

To whom are you talking?

'To' is the preposition and 'whom' is a **relative pronoun**. However, I'm sure you agree that the second example sounds very pompous; nowadays this 'rule' is often ignored.

Some other prepositions are: from, above, with, by, of, on, after, for, in and between.

Revising the points

- Adjectives describe nouns and add colour to your writing.

- They can be used singly or in a list.

- They can precede the noun or be placed after the verb.

- Adverbs modify or help verbs, adjectives or other adverbs.

- When modifying a verb, they usually end in '. . . ly'.

- Prepositions 'govern' nouns or pronouns.

PARAGRAPHING YOUR WORK

Structuring a paragraph
Look at the following example:

> Stark white and threatening, the letter lay on the brown door mat. I stared at it; my body became rigid. Although I hadn't seen it for years, I'd have recognised my sister's handwriting anywhere. Why was she writing to me now? Forcing my reluctant knees to bend, I stooped down and picked it up. Holding it as carefully as if it contained a time bomb, I carried it to the kitchen and dropped it on the table. Then, turning my back on it, I picked up the kettle with shaking hands and filled it. Hardly aware of what I was doing, I plugged it in and took a mug out of the cupboard. Still in a daze, I made the coffee and took some scalding sips. Then gingerly I picked up the envelope and slit it open. It was a wedding invitation! 'Mr and Mrs Collins' requested 'the pleasure of the company of Miss Cathy Singleton at the wedding of their daughter Lydia . . .' I dropped the card in amazement. Was my niece really old enough to be married? Had my sister at last decided to bury the hatchet or had Lydia forced her to send the invitation? I couldn't believe that I, the black sheep of the family, had actually been invited to the wedding of my estranged sister's daughter.

If you picked up a book and glanced at the page you've just read, you'd probably replace it on the shelf. Sentences have to be grouped together in **paragraphs** which are indented at the beginning so the page looks more 'reader friendly'.

Paragraphs can vary in length but each paragraph deals with

one topic. Within the group of sentences there should usually be a **topic sentence**; this is the main sentence and the content is expanded in the rest of the paragraph.

The positioning of the topic sentence can vary. Look at the following example. It is the first paragraph of the passage above. It is indented and the topic sentence, which is underlined, opens it. It introduces the letter and the following sentences are all related to it.

> Stark white and threatening, the letter lay on the brown door mat. I stared at it; my body became rigid. Although I hadn't seen it for years, I'd have recognised my sister's handwriting anywhere. Why was she writing to me now?

In the next example, which is the second paragraph of the original passage, the opening sentences build up to the final opening of the letter in the last sentence. In this case the topic sentence, underlined, comes last.

> Forcing my reluctant knees to bend, I stooped down and picked it up. Holding it as carefully as if it contained a time bomb, I carried it to the kitchen and dropped it on the table. Then, turning my back on it, I picked up the kettle with shaking hands and filled it. Hardly aware of what I was doing, I plugged it in and took a mug out of the cupboard. Still in a daze, I made the coffee and took some scalding sips. Then gingerly I picked up the envelope and slit it open.

There follows a short paragraph with the topic sentence underlined. The brevity of the paragraph emphasises Cathy's amazement at the wedding invitation. In the final paragraph the topic sentence is at the end as the narrator's amazement reaches a climax when she gives a reason for her astonishment.

> It was a wedding invitation! 'Mr and Mrs Collins' requested 'the pleasure of the company of Miss Cathy Singleton at the wedding of their daughter, Lydia . . . '
> I dropped the card in amazement. Was my niece really old enough to be married? Had my sister at last decided to bury the hatchet or had Lydia forced her to send the invitation? I couldn't believe that I, the black sheep of the family, had

actually been invited to the wedding of my estranged sister's daughter.

Single sentence paragraphs

Most paragraphs contain a number of sentences but it is possible to use a one-sentence paragraph for effect. Look at the following example:

> He heard the ominous sound of footsteps but suddenly he realised he had a chance. There was a key in the door. Swiftly he turned it in the lock before his captors could reach him. While the door handle rattled, he turned his attention to the window. There was a drainpipe nearby. Opening the window, he stretched out his hand and grasped it. Clambering over the windowsill, he started to slither down. A shout from below startled him.
>
> Losing his grip, he crashed to the ground at the feet of his enemy.

In this case the single sentence of the second paragraph is dramatic and stands out from the rest of the text.

Revising the points

● The start of a paragraph must always be indented.

● Paragraphs must deal with only one topic.

● Each paragraph should have a topic sentence whose content is expanded in the rest of the paragraph.

● Short paragraphs may be used for effect.

SETTING OUT DIRECT SPEECH

Direct speech is what a character actually says. When writing it, paragraphs are used slightly differently. You can tell at a glance how much direct speech is contained on a page because of the way in which it is set out.

Examples of direct speech

Look at the following passage:

'Cathy's accepted the invitation,' said Ruth.

'Oh good,' replied her husband. 'I hoped she would come.'

Ruth glared at him and snapped, 'I think she's got a cheek. When I think of all the trouble she caused, I can't believe it.'

'You invited her,' retorted Brian, looking amused.

'Only because Lydia wanted her to come.'

Ruth flounced out of the room, slamming the door. She was furious; she had been so sure her sister would refuse the invitation.

Notice that the speech itself is enclosed in **inverted commas** and there is always a single **punctuation mark** *before* they are closed. This is usually a **comma** unless it is the end of a sentence when it is, of course, a **full stop**. If a question is asked, a **question mark** is used. A new **paragraph** is always started at the beginning of the sentence which contains the speech.

'Cathy's accepted the invitation,' said Ruth.

'Why did you invite her?' asked Brian.

'I invited her because Lydia asked me to.'

Brian laughed and remarked, 'I'm glad she's coming. I always liked her.'

Ruth mocked, 'You were taken in by her.'

If a question mark is used, it replaces the comma as in the second sentence. In the fourth paragraph notice that the speech does *not* begin the sentence and Brian says *two* sentences before the inverted commas are closed. The first word of a person's speech always begins with a capital letter.

Revising the points

● Direct speech is always enclosed in inverted commas.

● A new paragraph always starts at the beginning of the sentence in which a character speaks.

● There is always a punctuation mark before the inverted commas are closed.

• A punctuation mark always separates the speech from the person who says it.

Interrupting direct speech

Sometimes a character's speech will be interrupted by 'she said' or something similar and in this case a new paragraph is not started because the same person is speaking:

> 'I don't know how you can be so calm,' she said. 'I am very upset.'

There is a **full stop** after 'said' because the first sentence had been completed. If it had not been completed, the **punctuation mark** should be a **comma** and the following speech starts with a small letter instead of a capital letter. Look at the following example:

> 'I do wish,' he sighed, 'that you wouldn't get so upset.'

There is a **comma** after 'sighed' and 'that' does not begin with a capital letter.

Returning to the narrative

When the speaker has finished speaking and the story or narrative is resumed, a new paragraph is started:

> 'You invited her,' retorted Brian.
>   Ruth flounced out of the room, slamming the door. She was furious; she had been so sure her sister would refuse the invitation.

Using quotation marks

Inverted commas are also used to enclose quotations and titles:

> She went to see the film 'Sense and Sensibility'.

> 'A stitch in time saves nine' is a famous proverb.

> The expression 'the mind's eye' comes from Shakespeare's play 'Hamlet'.

Notice that the **full stop** has been placed *outside* the **inverted** commas when the quotation or title is at the end of the sentence. It forms part of the sentence.

Avoiding confusion within speech

If a quotation or a title is used by someone who is speaking, use **double inverted commas** for the quotations to avoid confusion:

> 'I think the proverb "Too many cooks spoil the broth" is quite right,' David said crossly.
> 'I wanted to see "The Little Princess" but the last performance was yesterday,' Alison remarked sadly.
> 'Have you seen the film "Babe"?' asked John.
> 'No, but I'm going to see the new "Dr Who",' replied Sarah.

In the last two examples the titles are at the end of the speech so the **quotation marks** are closed first. These are followed by the **punctuation mark** and finally by the **inverted commas** which close the speech. (When work is typed, titles and quotations are usually shown in italics.)

Changing direct speech into indirect or reported speech

Indirect speech needs no **inverted commas** as the actual words are not used.

Direct speech
> 'Cathy's accepted the invitation,' said Ruth.

Indirect speech
> Ruth said that Cathy had accepted the invitation.

Direct speech
> 'I want to go to the town,' she said.

Indirect speech
> She said that she wanted to go to the town.

Notice that in both cases the **conjunction** 'that' has been used. In the second example the first person 'I' has been changed to the third person 'she'.

● Indirect speech needs no inverted commas.

- 'That' is added between 'said' and the reporting of the speech.

Setting out a play

When writing a play, inverted commas are not needed because only speech is used. The character's name is put at the side of the page and is followed by a **colon**. Stage directions for the actors are usually shown in italics or brackets:

RUTH: Cathy's accepted the invitation.
BRIAN: Oh good. I hoped she would come.
RUTH: (Glaring at him) I think she's got a cheek. When I think of all the trouble she caused, I can't believe it.
BRIAN: You invited her.
           (Ruth flounces out of the room, slamming the door.)

Revising the points

- The actual words said by a character are enclosed in inverted commas.

- A new paragraph must be started at the beginning of the sentence in which the person starts to speak.

- There is always a punctuation mark before the inverted commas are closed.

- Start a new paragraph when returning to the narrative.

- Use double inverted commas for quotations and titles.

- Inverted commas are not needed when reporting speech or writing a play.

CHECKLIST

- What is a **clause**?

- What is the purpose of a **personal pronoun**?

- Why should **nouns** agree?

- How are **conjunctions** used?

- List as many **conjunctions** as you can.

- What is a **phrase**?

- Define (a) an **adjective** and (b) an **adverb**.

- What purpose does a **paragraph** serve?

- When do you use **inverted commas**?

- How is a **play** set out?

PRACTISING WHAT YOU'VE LEARNT

1. Complete the following sentences:

(a) The harassed housewife . . . .
(b) Sarah . . . .
(c) Queen Victoria . . . .
(d) . . . . won the race.
(e) His cousin . . . .
(f) He . . . . to play tennis.
(g) The telephone . . . .
(h) He . . . . the computer.
(i) The castle . . . . a ruin.
(j) The dog . . . . John.

2. In the following passage replace the **nouns**, if necessary, with **pronouns**:

Sarah was working in her office. Sarah looked out of the window and saw the window cleaner. The windows were very dirty. The windows needed cleaning. Sarah asked the window cleaner if he had rung the front door bell. The window cleaner said he had. The window cleaner asked if Sarah wanted her windows cleaned. Sarah said she did want the windows cleaned. The window cleaner said the garden gate was unlocked. Sarah was sure she had locked the

garden gate. When the window cleaner rang the door bell
for the second time, Sarah heard the door bell.

3. Correct the following sentences:

(a) The Government are preparing to discuss the new Divorce Bill.
(b) That class are very noisy today.
(c) Everyone has done their work.
(d) The crowd were enthusiastic.

4. Add appropriate **conjunctions** or **relative pronouns** to the
   following passage and set it out in **paragraphs**:

> . . . it was so cold, Judith decided to play tennis at the club.
> Then she discovered . . . her tennis racquet, . . . was very
> old, had a broken string. . . . there was no time to have it
> mended, she knew she would not be able to play . . . she
> angrily threw the racquet across the room. It knocked over
> a china figurine . . . broke in half. She started to cry. . . .
> the telephone rang, she rushed to answer it . . . it was a
> wrong number. She picked up the broken china ornament.
> . . . she found some superglue, would she be able to mend
> it? . . . she broke it, she had forgotten how much she liked
> it. . . . she had nothing better to do, she decided to go to
> the town to buy some glue. . . . she was shopping, she met
> Dave . . . invited her to a party that evening. She was thrilled
> . . . she had been feeling very depressed.

5. Add suitable **phrases** to complete the following sentences.

(a) . . . . , he hurtled into the room.
(b) He broke his leg . . . .
(c) Mr Samson, ... , walked on to the stage.
(d) . . . . , she thought about the events of the day.
(e) . . . . , the child giggled.

6. Change the following examples of **direct speech** into **indirect
   speech**.

   'Will you come to the dance, Susan?' asked John.
   'I can't go because I'm going to a wedding,' replied Susan.

7. Set out the following dialogue as a **play**.

> 'I've got so much to do,' wailed Ruth.
> 'The wedding's not for ages,' Brian reminded her.
> 'But there's the food to order, the wedding cake to make and the dresses to buy.'
> She started to clear the table. Brian moved towards the door.
> 'I have to go to the office today. I'll be back for dinner,' he announced.
> 'Wait,' Ruth called. 'I want you to do some shopping for me. I've got a list somewhere.'

See page 127 for suggested answers.

DISCUSSION POINTS

1. Is it necessary to know the names of the different parts of speech?

2. Why are paragraphs necessary?

3. Do inverted commas serve a useful purpose?

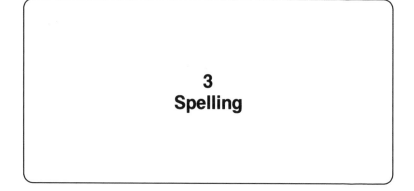

3
Spelling

ESTABLISHING THE GROUND RULES

English spelling is not easy to learn. There *are* some rules but often there are many exceptions to the rule. Some spellings and pronunciation appear to be illogical. It is therefore important that certain spellings are *learnt*.

There are twenty-six letters in our alphabet. Five are **vowels** and the rest are **consonants**.

Forming words

The **vowels** are A, E, I, O, U. All words have to contain at least one vowel ('y' is considered to be a vowel in words like 'rhythm' and 'psychology'). **Consonants** are all the other letters that are not vowels. So that a word can be pronounced easily, vowels are placed between them. No more than three consonants can be placed together. Below are two lists. The first contains some words with three consecutive consonants and in the second are words with two consecutive consonants:

(a) school, scream, chronic, Christian, through, splash.
(b) flap, grab, occasion, commander, baggage, added.

All the words in the examples have the consonants separated by vowels.

Forming plurals

To form a plural word an 's' is usually added to a **noun**. But there are some exceptions. If a noun ends in 'y', and there is a consonant before it, a plural is formed by changing the 'y' into an 'i' and adding '-es':

lady	→	ladies
berry	→	berries
company	→	companies
nappy	→	nappies

If the 'y' is preceded by another vowel, an 's' only is added:

monkey	→	monkeys
donkey	→	donkeys
covey	→	coveys

If a noun ends in 'o' and a consonant precedes the 'o', '-es' is added to form a plural

potato	→	potatoes
tomato	→	tomatoes
hero	→	heroes

If there is a vowel before the 'o', an 's' only is added.

studio	→	studios
zoo	→	zoos
patio	→	patios

Changing the form of a verb

When a **verb** ends in 'y' and it is necessary to change the tense by adding other letters, the 'y' is changed into an 'i' and 'es' or 'ed' is added.

He will <u>marry</u> her tomorrow.

He was <u>married</u> yesterday.

A dog likes to <u>bury</u> his bone.

A dog always <u>buries</u> his bone.

Adding 's' to 'awkward' words

It would be difficult to add an 's' only to some words because it would be impossible to pronounce them. These are words that end in 'ch', 'sh', 's', 'x' and 'z'. In this case an 'e' has to be added before the 's':

church	→	churches
brush	→	brushes
duchess	→	duchesses
buzz	→	buzzes

Using 'long vowels' and 'short' vowels

There is often a silent 'e' at the end of the word if the vowel is 'long':

date, bite, hope, late, dupe

Each of these words consists of one syllable (one unit of sound). If another syllable is added, the 'e' is removed:

date	→	dating
bite	→	biting
hope	→	hoping

If there is no 'e' at the end of a word, the vowel is usually short:

bit, hop, let

If a second syllable is added to these words, the consonant is usually doubled:

bit	→	bitten
hop	→	hopping
let	→	letting

There are, of course, some exceptions. If the 'e' is preceded by a 'g' or a 'c', the 'e' is usually retained. To remove it would produce a 'hard' sound instead of a 'soft' one:

marriage	→	marriageable
age	→	ageing
service	→	serviceable

Adding '-ly' to adjectives

When forming an **adverb** from an **adjective**, 'ly' (not 'ley') is added. If there is a 'y' at the end of the adjective, it must be changed to an 'i':

adjective	*adverb*
happy	happily
beautiful	beautifully
quick	quickly
slow	slowly

If a word ends in 'ic', '-ally' is added to it:

enthusiastic → enthusiastically

'I' before 'e' except after 'c'

This rule seems to have been made to be broken. Some words keep to it but others break it. Here are some that follow the rule. All of them are pronounced 'ee' – as in 'seed'.

no 'C' in front	*after 'C'*
niece	ceiling
piece	receive
grief	deceive

Exceptions to this rule are:

neighbours, vein, either, neither, seize, weird

AVOIDING COMMON MISTAKES

Because some words do not follow any rules, there are many words in the English language that are frequently misspelled. These words have to be learnt. Figure 2 is a list of the most common.

Avoiding confusion

Some words that are pronounced in the same way are spelt differently. These, too, have to be learnt in order to avoid mistakes. Can you find the mistakes in the following examples?

1. I no you are their.
2. I can sea to ships on the see.
3. Did you no there house is too be sold?
4. Hear is your packed lunch.
5. Their is a whole in your jacket.
6. You can go to London two.

surprise	disappear	disappoint	lonely
independence	separate	receive	thief
excitement	usage	journey	island
vehicle	already	jewellery	vicious
immediately	weird	ceiling	label
womb	collar	deceive	league
yield	desperate	language	said
lightning	tried	paid	frightening
eighth	maintenance	envelope	precious
centre	except	preferred	massacre
accept	privilege	metaphor	exhibition
doubt	simile	exhaust	secretary
miniature	though	familiar	scissors
misspell	fierce	sergeant	niece
grief	similar	occasion	idle
spaghetti	parallel	idol	subtle

Fig. 2. Commonly misspelled words.

7. The teacher kept in the hole class.
8. The violinist took a bough.
9. Because of the wind, the bow of the tree broke.
10. She passed threw the crowd.

11. He through the ball.
12. Know milk was left today.

There are 18 mistakes. Did you find them all? Here is the correct version:

1. I <u>know</u> you are <u>there.</u>
2. I can <u>see</u> <u>two</u> ships on the <u>sea.</u>
3. Did you <u>know</u> <u>their</u> house is <u>to</u> be sold?
4. <u>Here</u> is your packed lunch.
5. <u>There</u> is a <u>hole</u> in your jacket.
6. You can go to London <u>too.</u>
7. The teacher kept in the <u>whole</u> class.
8. The violinist took a <u>bow.</u>
9. Because of the wind, the <u>bough</u> of the tree broke.
10. She passed <u>through</u> the crowd.
11. He <u>threw</u> the ball.
12. <u>No</u> milk was left today.

USING A DICTIONARY

Checking your spelling
Use a dictionary frequently to check your spelling. Don't guess the spelling of a word. Look it up. It is helpful to keep a list of words that you have misspelled so you can learn them.

Looking at words
A dictionary not only tells you how to spell a word. It also tells you what part of speech the word is. Sometimes the word appears more than once as it has different meanings and can be used as a different part of speech. Look at the following examples:

land (noun)	(a)	The solid part of the earth
	(b)	A country
land (verb)	(c)	To go ashore or bring a plane down to the ground
fast (verb)	(a)	Abstain from eating
fast (noun)	(b)	The act of going without food

fast (adjective)   (c)   Firmly attached
fast (adverb)   (d)   Quickly

Identifying letters

You will have noticed that in a dictionary, letters after the word identify the part of speech:

n. = noun   a. = adjective   adv. = adverb   v. = verb

You will find that the verb is often followed by 't' or 'i'. 'v.t.' stands for **verb transitive**. A transitive verb takes an object when used in a sentence. We will use the verb 'to write' as an example:

He wrote a letter.

The 'object' of the verb 'wrote' is 'letter'. It is, of course, a noun.

'v.i.' stands for **verb intransitive**. This means that the verb does not take an object. Many verbs can be used both transitively *and* intransitively. The following example uses the verb 'to write' intransitively:

She writes beautifully.

In this case no noun or 'object' follows the verb 'writes' so here it is used intransitively.

Exploring the dictionary

The dictionary will often give the derivation of a word. English is a rich language that owes much to other languages. Some words like 'rendezvous' are obviously French and have been kept in their original forms. Others like 'galley' have been adapted from several languages.

If you have time, browse through a dictionary looking at the derivation of some of our words. It can be a fascinating and rewarding experience.

MAKING USE OF THE THESAURUS

A thesaurus can also be very useful. It will help you to find an alternative word (**synonym**) for a word that you have used too much. Words are shown alphabetically and beside each will be a list of words that could replace the word you want to lose. Of course, not all the synonyms will be suitable. It will depend on the context of the word.

Roget's Thesaurus

This is the most famous and has two main sections. The second part lists words alphabetically and identifies the parts of speech. After the words are numbers. These refer to the first part where the synonyms for the different parts of speech will be given.

Other thesauri

There are many smaller versions including pocket ones and these can be found in most bookshops.

Adding to your vocabulary

Using a thesaurus is an excellent way of adding to your vocabulary. It is useful to keep a list of words that you have found so that you can use them again and in this way increase your knowledge. Here is a list of synonyms that could be used instead of the overworked adjective 'nice':

> pleasant, attractive, delicious, agreeable, enjoyable, delightful, pleasing

CHECKLIST

● What are **vowels** and what is their purpose?

● What are some of the basic **spelling rules**?

● To what uses can a **dictionary** be put?

● What is a **thesaurus** and what is its purpose?

PRACTISING WHAT YOU'VE LEARNT

1. What is the plural form of the following words?

   lady, company, monkey, tomato, boa, princess, dance

2. Add '-ing' to the following words:

    dine, live, hit, hop, skip, write, mate, mine

3. Form **adverbs** from the following **adjectives:**

    happy, joyful, kind, angry, wonderful, clear, quick, careless

4. In the following passage fill in the missing words.

    . . . were no ships on the . . . that morning. She could . . . the
    white foam as the waves crashed on the shore. She would . . .
    when . . . car arrived as it would drive . . . the gate. Idly, she
    . . . a stone into the . . . . The . . . of the trees on the cliff . . .
    swaying in the wind. It was . . . cold . . . sit still. Kicking off
    her sandals, she noticed she had . . . holes in her socks. She
    had intended to . . . her new ones. Her hair ribbon had also
    come undone and crossly she tied it in a bow and stood up,
    holding her shoes. . . . she could . . . the car.

5. What do the following letters stand for?

    n.   v.t.   v.i.   a.   adv.

6. Find synonyms for the underlined words in the following
    passage:

    It was a nice day so the children decided to have a picnic. They
    walked along the cliff path and climbed down to the beach.
    The waves crashed on the shore as they ate their pleasant lunch.

See page 128 for suggested answers.

DISCUSSION POINTS

1. Why is it important to establish the ground rules for spelling?

2. Why is keeping a record of 'new' words important?

3. Do you use a dictionary frequently? Have you found a
    thesaurus helpful?

4
Apostrophes and Abbreviations

USING APOSTROPHES TO SHOW POSSESSION

Apostrophes are put at the end of **nouns** when the nouns have something belonging to them.

Making a singular noun possessive
If a noun is singular and it has something belonging to it, add an apostrophe and an 's'. For singular words that show possession the apostrophe is always placed *before* the 's':

Karen's handbag was stolen.

Her neighbour's fence was blown down.

The child's ball bounced over the wall.

If the singular noun already ends in an 's', another 's' should still be added:

The princess's bridal gown was made by a well-known couturier.

The thief stole the duchess's jewels

However, in some cases the extra 's' can be omitted as in the following examples:

James' book was missing.

He damaged his Achilles' tendon.

Making a plural noun possessive

Most nouns add an 's' to make a plural. In this case the apostrophe goes *after* the noun if it is possessive.

> The thundering of the horses' hoofs broke the silence.

> The ladies' gowns were beautiful.

Some nouns do not add an 's' to become a plural. In this case, if they are possessive, they are treated like singular nouns. The apostrophe is added *before* the extra 's'. Some of these words are: children, men, women, mice, geese, sheep.

> The children's playground was vandalised.

> Kate watched the mice's tails disappearing round the corner.

> The men's club room was being redecorated.

> The sale of women's coats was postponed.

Using possessive pronouns correctly

When using the possessive form of a pronoun, apostrophes are *not* used. The **possessive pronouns** are: mine, hers, his, its, ours, yours and theirs.

> The blame is <u>mine</u>. (no apostrophe)

> These books are <u>hers</u>. (no apostrophe)

> The first prize was <u>his</u>. (no apostrophe)

> <u>Theirs</u> was the glory. (no apostrophe)

> The success was <u>ours</u>. (no apostrophe)

> That house is <u>theirs</u>. (no apostrophe)

Note especially
> The cat cleaned its whiskers.

> *not*

> The cat cleaned it's whiskers.

● 'Its' possessive does *not* use an apostrophe.

- 'It's' is used only when letters are omitted.

- 'It's' means 'it is' or 'it has'.

Revising the points
- The apostrophe is placed before the 's' if the noun is singular.

- The apostrophe is placed after the 's' if the noun is plural.

- Add an 's' and put the apostrophe before it if the plural does not end in 's'.

- Do not use an apostrophe when using a possessive pronoun.

- Remember 'its' possessive does not use an apostrophe.

ABBREVIATING WORDS

When writing formally, it is better not to abbreviate. Write the words out in full. However, it is, of course, acceptable to abbreviate when writing dialogue.

Using apostrophes to abbreviate words
An **abbreviation** is when letters are missed out. Sometimes two words are combined into one. An apostrophe is placed where the letter or letters have been omitted:

'Do not'	→	'don't'
'Can not'	→	'can't'
'Would not'	→	'wouldn't'

Note especially
   'Could have' becomes 'could've'

   not 'could of'

Because of the way the abbreviation in the above example sounds, a common mistake is to use the word 'of' instead of the abbreviation ''ve'.

The abbreviation of 'have' is ''ve' *not* 'of'.

Abbreviating words without using apostrophes

When words are shortened, it is usual to put a **full stop** at the end:

information	info.
document	doc.
etcetera	etc.
abbreviation	abbr.
adjective	adj.
language	lang.

The names of **counties** are shortened in the following way and all need full stops after them:

Berkshire	Berks.
Nottinghamshire	Notts.
Gloucestershire	Glos.
Oxfordshire	Oxon.
Hampshire	Hants.

Other words that are often abbreviated are **titles** but some of these should only be abbreviated if the title is followed by the person's full name. A full stop should be put after the abbreviation if it is used.

Capt. Edward Symes

not

Capt. Symes

Rev. Steven Reynolds

not

Rev. Reynolds

HANDLING CONTRACTIONS

Some words are abbreviated by using the first and last letters only. These are **contractions** of the original word and do not usually need a full stop at the end:

Mister	Mr
Mistress	Mrs
Doctor	Dr
Road	Rd
Street	St
Saint	St

No full stop is needed after a contraction.

USING ACRONYMS

It is becoming increasingly common to describe companies or organisations only by the initial letters of the name of the group. This is called an **acronym**. This is now so prevalent that we often forget what the original letters stood for! It is no longer considered necessary to put a full stop after each capital letter. Here are some reminders of frequently used acronyms:

RADA	Royal Academy of Dramatic Arts
NATO	North Atlantic Treaty Organisation
ASH	Action on Smoking and Health
UNICEF	United Nations Children's Fund
RAF	Royal Air Force
AIDS	Acquired Immune Deficiency Syndrome
LAMDA	London Academy of Music and Dramatic Art

Revising the points

- Use an apostrophe if letters are omitted to abbreviate words.
- Remember the abbreviation of 'have' is ''ve' not 'of'.
- Put a full stop after shortened or abbreviated words.
- Do not put a full stop after contractions or in acronyms.

CHECKLIST

- What is the purpose of **apostrophes** and when are they used?
- When are **full stops** used after **abbreviations**?
- When should you *not* abbreviate?
- What is an **acronym**? How is it written?

PRACTISING WHAT YOU'VE LEARNT

1. Put **apostrophes** in the following passage:

> Carefully he picked up Johns bundle. It wasnt very heavy. He glanced warily at the caves entrance. It was very dark. The picnic baskets still lay where theyd been thrown. He stepped into the cave and almost fell over a pile of little rubber tubes that looked like mices tails. Inside there was a boulder of rock. Its smooth surface glistened like gold. Davids hands shook. He wished hed stayed with his brothers. His parents quarrel had upset him and that was why hed run away. In a weeks time they were going on holiday. He wished now that hed stayed at home as hed been told.

2. Correct the following passage, inserting **full stops** where necessary:

> The foll doc from Mrs Barker gives info about the lectures to be given by Prof Peter Coombs in Sept and Oct in St Margaret's Church Hall. The Hall is in Church Rd and is situated near the station. Prof Peter Coombs will be accompanied by Dr Martin.

See page 129 for suggested answers.

DISCUSSION POINTS

1. How necessary is it to use apostrophes in the right place?

2. Is the full stop important when abbreviating?

3. What purpose do acronyms serve?

5
Correct English

RECOGNISING COMMON MISTAKES

Revising punctuation

Remember that punctuation is essential if your work is to make sense.

- Do not use commas instead of full stops. If in doubt, put a full stop.

- Remember to put a question mark at the end of a question.

Can you find the mistakes in the following?

> He was in a hurry, he quickly pushed the newspaper into the rubbish bin, Maria watched him, what was he doing.

Here is the correct version:

> He was in a hurry. He quickly pushed the newspaper into the rubbish bin. Maria watched him. What was he doing?

Revising sentence construction

Remember that sentences must make sense. Each sentence must contain at least one subject (**noun**) and one **verb**. If there is more than one verb, there are two **clauses** and these should either be separated by a **full stop** or **semi-colon** or linked by a **conjunction**. There are three clauses in the following piece but they are not linked:

> He crept round the corner she followed him she was very suspicious.

61

There are several ways in which this could be corrected:

> As he crept round the corner, she followed him; she was very suspicious.

> He crept round the corner; she followed him because she was very suspicious.

> As he crept round the corner, she followed him because she was very suspicious.

Revising the correct use of verbs

Always make sure that the **nouns** and the **verbs** 'agree'. If the noun is singular, the verb should also be singular.

> Remember that **collective nouns** are singular and are followed by the singular form of the verb.

> The government is hoping to win the vote of confidence.

> *not*

> The government are hoping to win the vote of confidence.

Avoiding the misuse of pronouns

There is often confusion in the use of the words: 'I' and 'me', 'she' and 'her', 'he' and 'him', 'we' and 'us', 'they' and 'them'.

'I', 'she', 'he', 'we' and 'they' are **personal pronouns** and are usually the **subject** of the sentence. That means they are the instigators of the action in the sentence:

> I like travelling.

> She went on holiday.

> He has been made redundant.

> We have no milk.

> They are moving today.

'Me', 'her', 'him', 'us' and 'them' are usually the **objects** of the sentence. That means that something is 'done' to them:

The ball struck <u>me</u>.

The prize was given to <u>her</u>.

The tree fell on <u>him</u>.

The audience applauded <u>us</u>.

The teacher scolded <u>them</u>.

Confusion often arises when there is a name as well as the pronoun. It is sometimes thought that 'I' sounds better than 'me' but it is actually incorrect:

Tracy and <u>I</u> are going to London.

not

<u>Tracy</u> and <u>me</u> are going to London.

Mrs Jones gave some sweets to John and <u>me</u>.

not

Mrs Jones gave some sweets to John and <u>I</u>.

To check which is correct, it is often useful to remove the proper noun. The following examples are obviously wrong, aren't they?

Mrs Jones gave some sweets to I.

Me is going to London

- 'I', 'he', 'she', 'we' and 'they' are **subjects** and are usually at the beginning of the sentence.
- 'Me', 'her', 'him', 'us' and 'them' are **objects** and usually follow the **verb**.

However, when a **verb** is 'understood' at the end of the sentence, it is the **personal pronoun** that is used:

He is taller than <u>I</u> (am).

She was angrier than <u>he</u> (was).

Neither 'am' nor 'was' needs to be included at the end of the sentences. They are both 'understood'. The following examples are therefore incorrect:

> He is taller than <u>me</u>.

> She was angrier than <u>him</u>.

If the verb was added instead of being 'understood', it would sound quite wrong, wouldn't it? Say the following aloud and you'll see what I mean:

> He was taller than me am.

> She was angrier than him was.

Revising spelling

● Learn the most commonly misspelled words; for example:

> surprise, disappear, disappoint, independent

● Learn the correct spelling of words that sound the same but are spelt differently; for example:

hear	–	here		
their	–	there		
sea	–	see		
too	–	two	–	to

The words 'practise' and 'practice' are often confused and so are 'advise' and 'advice'. 'Practise' and 'advise' are the **verbs** and 'practice' and 'advice' are the **nouns**:

> You must **practise** the piano if you are to improve.

> There is a cricket **practice** in the nets today.

> I **advise** you to behave yourself.

> She always refused to take **advice**.

> The **verb** has an 's' before the 'e'. The **noun** has a 'c' before the 'e'.

Other words that are often confused are 'council' and 'counsel'. 'compliment' and 'complement', 'principle' and 'principal' and 'stationery' and 'stationary'.

Council/counsel
1. A **council** (*noun*) is an administrative group which has power to make decisions.
2. A **councillor** (*noun*) sits on a **council** (*noun*).
3. To **counsel** (*verb*) someone is to help them by listening to them and giving them advice.
4. A **counsellor** (*noun*) **counsels** (*verb*) clients.

Compliment/complement
1. A **compliment** (*noun*) is an expression of praise.
2. 'He paid me a **compliment** today.'
3. To **complement** (*verb*) means to complete the whole.
4. 'Your scarf **complements** that dress beautifully.'

Principal/principle
1. A **principal** (*noun*) is the Head of a College.
2. 'The **Principal** was very pleased with the students' work.'
3. **Principal** can also be an **adjective** meaning main or chief.
4. 'The **Principal** Boy in the pantomime was played by Joan.'
5. A **principle** (*noun*) is the standard you maintain.
6. 'In spite of difficulties, she always kept to her **principles**.'

Stationery/stationary
1. A **stationer** (*noun*) sells writing paper so **stationery** (*noun*) is writing paper and envelopes.
2. 'I ran out of **stationery** so I had to buy some.'
3. **Stationary** (*adjective*) means fixed in one place.
4. 'The train was **stationary** at the platform.'

Avoiding common mistakes
A mistake that is frequently heard is the following:

He is very different <u>to</u> his brother.

This is wrong. It should be:

He is very different <u>from</u> his brother.

If you **differ**, you move away **from**.
If you are **similar**, you are similar **to**.

Avoiding mistakes when using apostrophes and abbreviations

● Do not put an apostrophe every time there is a plural word ending in 's'.

● The abbreviation of 'could have' is 'could've' *not* 'could of'.

● Do not put a full stop after a contraction:

Doctor   →   Dr
Mister   →   Mr

AVOIDING UNNECESSARY REPETITION

● Remember that **nouns** do not usually need to be repeated within the same sentence.

● Replace them with **pronouns**:

He tried on his new boots. The boots were too tight.

This should be:

He tried on his new boots. <u>They</u> were too tight.

Avoiding tautologies

A tautology is where the same thing is said twice over in different ways, for example:

The last chapter will be at the end of the book.

The people applauded by clapping their hands.

These two sentences are repetitious. 'The last chapter' will obviously be at the end so it is not necessary to say so. 'Applause' is usually shown by clapping so 'by clapping their hands' is unnecessary.

Varying the sentence
If sentences frequently begin with the same word, the work becomes monotonous. Avoid the temptation to start consecutive sentences in the same way.

> She cautiously opened the door. She saw who stood on the doorstep so she hurriedly closed it. She ran back to the dining room. She started to cry. She was distraught.

These five sentences all start with 'she' so the passage does not flow. Is the following example better?

> Cautiously opening the door, Tina saw who stood on the doorstep so she hurriedly closed it. Running back to the dining room, the child started to cry. She was distraught.

The first two sentences and the third and fourth sentences have been combined and only the last sentence starts with 'she'. Two of the **pronouns** have been replaced with **nouns**. The writing is much 'tighter'.

MAKING COMPARISONS

When using **adjectives** to compare two things or people '-er' is usually added to the base word:

big	bigger
tall	taller
slow	slower
happy	happier

She is taller than I am.

He is slower than she is.

When more than two things or people are involved, '-est' is added to the adjective:

big	bigger	biggest
tall	taller	tallest
slow	slower	slowest
happy	happier	happiest

Adrian is the biggest of all the boys.

Mary is the tallest of the four girls.

Some words are so constructed that to add the suffix '-er' or '- est' would produce clumsy words. In this case 'more' and 'most' are put before the adjective instead:

beautiful	more beautiful	most beautiful
intelligent	more intelligent	most intelligent
irritable	more irritable	most irritable
excitable	more excitable	most excitable

Joanne was the most beautiful girl Frank had ever seen.

Gail was the most intelligent student in the class.

> 'More' and 'most' cannot be used if '-er' or '-est' have been used.

'Good', 'bad' and 'little' do not follow the rules and have their own words for comparison:

good	better	best
bad	worse	worst
little	less	least

The patient is <u>worse</u> today.

Clive is the <u>best</u> pupil I have ever taught.

That is the <u>least</u> of my worries.

ELIMINATING JARGON

The origin of 'jargon'
The word 'jargon' derives from a Middle English word meaning 'meaningless chatter'. The derivation suggests a very good reason why jargon should be avoided. Anyone who is a member of a group uses jargon that is intelligible only to other members of the same group. Lawyers have their own jargon and so do politicians, schoolteachers and nurses.

Using jargon today
Today we are bombarded with words ending in 'ise'. Privatise, normalise, prioritise, nationalise are all words that are now embedded in our language. But they are jargon and should be avoided as should all forms of jargon. Use words and expressions that will be easily understood by anyone who reads your work. Strive always for originality and simplicity in your writing. Look at the following example:

> The local council is producing a programme to normalise the work experience schedule of students in its employ. Any input from department heads to finalise this should be submitted by the due date.

It's full of jargon, isn't it? But it is an internal note so should be understood by its readers. What about the following example?

> Louis had fed in the appropriate information before finalising his entry. Now he hurtled along the race track hoping to maximise his potential.

This sounds very pompous. Here is the simplified version:

> Louis had given all the appropriate information before entering the race. Now he hurtled along the track, hoping to win.

Avoid jargon. Aim for simplicity.

STIMULATING YOUR IMAGINATION

Avoiding clichés

Clichés are phrases that are heard over and over again. We all use them and they are often very apt. Of course, they were original when they were said for the first time. Many of their origins have been lost but a number owe their existence to the Bible and Shakespeare. I'm sure some of the following expressions are familiar to you although the original words have sometimes been changed slightly:

> All that glistens (glisters) is not gold. (*Merchant of Venice*, Shakespeare)
>
> My mind's eye. (*Hamlet*, Shakespeare)
>
> Don't hide your light under a bushel. (The Bible)

Here are some more common examples:

> He stopped dead in his tracks.
>
> She went as white as a sheet.
>
> He ran like the wind.

The last two examples are very familiar although perhaps the middle one has lost its relevance as sheets no longer need be white.

Creating similes

'White as a sheet' and 'ran like the wind' are **similes**. These are comparisons between two things using the words 'like' or 'as', Many clichés are similes and they are often very vivid. However, they are not original and you should avoid them. It is much better to create your own 'images' so that your reader will be struck by the originality of your writing. If you want to create a simile using a colour, try to think of something unusual that is that colour.

The face of someone who is seasick might be said to be 'as green as grass' but 'as green as the mould at the bottom of an unwashed milk bottle' is far more original if not very pleasant.

'My legs felt like jelly' is not original although it is apt. The following suggests the same feeling but is more vivid because it is 'new':

My legs felt like spaghetti that had just been dipped into boiling water.

Using metaphors

Metaphors are also comparisons but they are 'implied' and do not use 'like' or 'as'. We use metaphorical language a great deal in everyday speech. It is language that is not literally true but cannot be classified as a lie as everyone knows what is meant. Look at the following examples:

I'm starving.

He says he's freezing.

She's dying of thirst.

All are clichés and all are metaphors. The language is **metaphorical** – not literally true. If it were true, all three characters would be dead and we know that is not what is meant.

The following is a **metaphor**:

The moon is a silver ball in the dark sky.

but if 'like' is added, it becomes a **simile**:

The moon is like a silver ball in the dark sky.

Metaphors and **similes** both add interest to your writing but they should be used sparingly.

Personifying inanimate objects

To **personify** means to give an inanimate object human characteristics. Look at the following examples:

The sun walked across the sky in her golden shoes.

The table groaned under the weight of the food.

Both use **personification**. The sun 'walks' and wears 'golden shoes'. The table 'groans'. They are also **metaphors** as they are not literally true.

The use of the **figures of speech** we have just discussed is common in prose writing and adds to the interest. 'Prose' is written and spoken language that does not have a regular beat or rhyme as some poetry does.

Revising the points

- Clichés are frequently used phrases. Avoid them.

- A simile is a comparison using 'like' or 'as'.

- A metaphor is an implied comparison without the use of 'like' or 'as'.

- Personification gives human characteristics to things that are not human.

IMPROVING YOUR STYLE

Economising on words

Good writing is simple and easy to understand. Unnecessary words should be eliminated. If one word can replace four, use it. Look at the following 'wordy' example:

> All of a sudden, he ran quickly to the computer. He knew it was absolutely essential to eliminate completely his very unique work which, although extremely excellent, could put him in bad danger. In the event that his enemies found and discovered what he had done, he would try to give advance warning of the catastrophic disaster that would follow.

A number of the words and phrases in this example are **tautologies**. They repeat what has already been said and are quite unnecessary. 'Unique' and 'excellent' cannot be qualified. They stand alone. Other expressions could be shortened to make the work flow. The passage could be tightened up by the removal of many extra words. Why use 'all of a sudden' when 'suddenly' will do? 'Eliminate' and 'essential' do not need to be qualified. 'Absolutely', 'completely', 'very', and 'extremely' therefore should be deleted. 'Bad danger', 'advance warning' and 'catastrophic disaster' are also wrong. 'Danger' *is* 'bad', a 'warning' always refers to the future and a 'disaster' *is* 'catastrophic'. Look at the revised version:

Suddenly, he rushed to the computer. He knew it was essential to eliminate his unique work, which, although excellent, could put him in danger. If his enemies discovered what he had done, he would try to give warning to the world of the disaster that would follow.

Using the active voice

The **active voice** is more positive than the **passive voice**. In the active voice a subject does something. In the passive voice something is done to him.

Active voice

> The father struck his son.
>
> The teacher gave the class a detention.

Passive voice

> The son was struck by his father.
>
> The class was given a detention by the teacher.

In the second version there are two extra words and I'm sure you'll agree that the first sentences have more vigour.

Avoiding negatives

Using positive statements instead of negative ones also economises on words. For example:

> He did not remember his wife's birthday.
>
> Clare was not present in the afternoon.

would be better as the following:

> He forgot his wife's birthday.
>
> Clare was absent in the afternoon.

Avoid double negatives which make a positive:

There isn't no one there.

I haven't got no lunch.

The 'not' and the 'no' cancel each other out and therefore the first example means there *is* someone there and the second means I *have* got some lunch.

There is a choice of two correct versions. Only *one* negative should be used if the sense is to be kept:

There isn't anyone there.

or

There is no one there.

I haven't got any lunch.

or

I have no lunch.

> Avoid double negatives.

Clarifying your work

Always check your work to make sure that it makes sense. Avoid vagueness and expressions which add nothing to your sentence. Some expressions to be avoided are: 'to tell you the truth', 'in fact', 'actually'.

> Avoid clichés, jargon, tautologies and unnecessary words.

Make sure your **phrases** and **clauses** are in the right order so there is no confusion:

She put the letter on the desk which had been opened.

In the above, 'which had been opened' refers to the letter not the desk so it should follow 'letter'. The following is the correct version:

She put the letter, which had been opened, on the desk.

Here's another example:

The knife was very sharp which he used.

The correct version is:

The knife, which he used, was very sharp.

Developing your own style
Now that you have a thorough grasp of the basics, you should aim to develop your own individual style of writing. Read widely so you can appreciate others' writing but do not copy them. Always check your work carefully to make sure your sentences make sense, are well-constructed and do not contain any careless mistakes.

Avoiding repetition
Avoid repeatedly using words like 'and', 'very', 'nice' and 'got'. All of them are very overworked. Change your sentence structure or find a **synonym** to replace them. Don't begin sentences with 'and', 'but' or 'also'.

Varying your sentences
Nothing is more monotonous than the repetition of the same sentence pattern. Vary it by changing the length of your sentences and by placing clauses and phrases in a different order. There is a variety of different sentence structures you can use. Look at the following examples:

1. The bride looked radiant. (One **main clause.**)

2. The match was cancelled because of the weather. (**Main clause** followed by **dependent** clause.)

3. Because of the weather, the match was cancelled. (**Dependent clause** followed by **main clause.**)

4. Peeping into the bedroom, she saw that her daughter was still asleep. (**Phrase** followed by **main clause.**)

5. The Crown Prince, who should have succeeded his father on

the throne, was assassinated last week. (**Dependent clause** inserted in the middle of a **main clause**.)

6. I had a shower, put on my new evening dress, dabbed some perfume behind my ears, picked up my handbag and rushed downstairs. (List of **main clauses** with subject 'I' 'understood'.)

7. Julie was playing the piano, Mark was doing his homework, Colin was in the kitchen and Karen was reading her library book. (List of **main clauses** each with a different subject.)

These are just a few of the sentence variations you can use.

●   Remember to use commas when more than one clause is used unless the conjunction is in the middle of the sentence.

●   Always check your work.

CHECKLIST

●   Avoid unnecessary repetition and **tautologies**.

●   Check **spellings** of frequently misspelled words.

●   Vary your **sentence structure**.

●   Avoid the use of **jargon** and **clichés**.

●   Use **similes** and **metaphors** to 'colour' your language.

●   Delete **unnecessary words**.

PRACTISING WHAT YOU'VE LEARNT

1. Correct the following:

    (a) The school are hoping to raise enough money to build a new drama studio.

    (b) He gave packages to both John and I.

    (c) Me and June is going out.

(d) The cat licked it's whiskers while the dogs' ate there dinner.

(e) Her work was very excellent.

(f) He hasn't got no coat.

(g) She could of gone to London.

2. Stimulate your imagination by creating **similes** or **metaphors** to describe the following:

(a) The sun setting over the sea.

(b) Thick fog.

(c) An empty room.

(d) A worried woman.

See page 129 for suggested answers.

DISCUSSION POINTS

1. Why is it necessary to vary your sentence structure?

2. Why should you develop your own style?

3. What is the purpose of similes and metaphors?

Part Two: English in Action
6
Writing an Essay and a Short Story

RESEARCHING YOUR ESSAY

Using the title
If you are planning your own title, make sure you deal with only one aspect of a subject. Don't make the subject too broad. If you are given a title, make sure you fully understand it before starting work. Remember that the titles of some essays can cover several lines and more than one sentence.

Example: GCSE Literature question
> Lady Macbeth was a complex character who dominated her husband. With detailed reference to the text, show how she achieved her aims.

During both your preparatory work and the actual writing of the essay, it is essential that you refer frequently to the title so that you are not tempted to wander off the point.

Think about the following:

- What is the title asking you to do?

- Are there two parts to the question?

- What research do you need to do?

- What are the key words in the title?

Researching the material
The most obvious place to start your research is the library. Here you will find books on all topics classified by subject, magazines, newspapers and also archive material. Some of this may be on disc. Archive material is very useful if you wish to use 'primary sources'

as they are called. These are original letters, diaries, books and periodicals. Librarians are usually very helpful so do ask if you are having difficulty finding something.

Visiting and interviewing

You may need to visit places and people to learn more about your topic. 'Experts' in their fields are usually very happy to be interviewed provided they are given plenty of notice. It is also courteous to write a thank-you note afterwards. Make sure your questions are relevant and you have written them down.

MAKING NOTES

Avoid copying down huge chunks of material. If you do, you might regurgitate it in your essay and be accused of **plagiarism** (passing someone else's work off as your own). It will always be obvious to the marker when the work is not yours. To safeguard against this always 'translate' the original into your own words. Of course, you are entitled to quote directly from the text but in this case you must put quotation marks around the quote and acknowledge its source. (See Chapter 2.)

Keeping it brief

Briefly write down the facts that you will need to use. If there are examples from a particular text that you may need, make a note of the book and the page number so that you can refer back to it. Use headings for your notes as this makes it easier when you start to write the essay.

Making a bibliography

Remember to keep a record of the books you use as you are usually required to identify your sources. Write a list of the books you have used stating the title, author, publisher and publication date. This is called a **bibliography** (or **references**).

Making your own notes

Sometimes your essay will not need any research. Perhaps you are sitting an examination and therefore have all the facts in your head; it might be a personal experience piece or something that you have to work out for yourself. Whatever type of writing you are doing you *must* make notes first. Write down quickly all the things that come into your head relating to the title. Sentences are not important at the moment. Words or phrases are sufficient. Your brain works faster than your pen and it is important to get everything down before you forget it.

PLANNING YOUR WORK

After your note-taking, it is essential to plan your essay. Your notes do *not* constitute the plan. They have to be organised.

Organising your notes

Your work should be set out in **paragraphs** and each paragraph will deal with one topic (see Chapter 2). From your notes you must decide how you can group your points so that the essay will flow naturally from one paragraph to the next. How you arrange your plan is up to you but remember to keep to the point. Use evidence to support what you say and explain why your quotations or references are relevant.

Remember that you must have an **introductory paragraph** showing what you are intending to do in your essay. The main body of the essay follows. From your notes pick out the main points that you will use and organise them under paragraph **headings**. Remember that a paragraph deals with one main idea but you may be able to group several similar points together. The **concluding paragraph** sums up the essay and shows that you have completed what you set out to do.

STRUCTURING YOUR ESSAY

Decide the best way to approach your essay. This will depend upon what type of essay you are writing.

- Is it going to be a piece of narrative told chronologically?

- Will it be a descriptive piece?

- Will you be expounding a theory and supporting it with your research?

- Will it be discursive? In this case both sides of an argument are used and you must write a balanced essay with evidence supporting both points of view.

Paragraph 1
Introduction.

Paragraph 2
Shows her opinion of Macbeth by her response to his letter.
Her cruel delight at the King's prospective visit.
Her domination of Macbeth when he enters.

Paragraph 3
She mocks Macbeth for his cowardice.
Shows herself to be without womanly feelings.
Forces him to do her will.
Berates him when he returns with the bloody knives.
Continues to mock him for his fear.

Paragraph 4
Banquet scene.
Reminds Macbeth of his duties.
Covers for him when he sees the ghost.
Berates him in private for his behaviour.

Paragraph 5
Summing up of ways she dominates.
She mocks him.
Her own actions.
Forces him to do her will.

Paragraph 6
Conclusion.

Fig. 3. Essay plan.

Figure 3 is a suggested plan for the Lady Macbeth essay: 'Lady Macbeth was a complex character who dominated her husband. With detailed reference to the text, show how she achieved her aims.'

WRITING YOUR ESSAY

Having done your plan, you are now ready to start writing.

Keeping to the point

Make sure you keep to the point by referring frequently to the title. Always keep it in front of you as you write. Make sure that your essay flows naturally from one paragraph to the next.

Producing a good opening

Your opening sentence is very important because it will either stimulate the reader to read on or put him off. It should be concise so the reader can understand what you are saying. You should aim to interest your reader from the beginning. Sometimes it is a good idea to start with a question – perhaps a controversial one. Look at the following two examples:

> Was Lady Macbeth a complex woman who dominated her husband?

> Did Lady Macbeth murder Duncan?

The first example leads the reader towards the discussion of the title. The second one would be more appropriate for a more philosophical discussion of the actual murder. Lady Macbeth did not actually stab Duncan but she definitely incited her husband to do so.

Ending your essay

In your final paragraph draw all the loose ends together and bring your essay to a logical conclusion. Make sure that you have already mentioned the points to which you are referring. Don't introduce new material in the last paragraph.

PLOTTING A SHORT STORY

Although you will probably not need to do any research if you are writing a short story, it is still important to plan your work carefully.

Planning the story

Write down an outline of the main events of your story in chronological order. Then decide where the story is to begin and how it is to develop. Will the events lead to an inevitable conclusion or will you use the 'twist-in-the-tale' device? The unexpected ending can be very effective if well done.

Avoiding detailed description

There will not be room for any detailed description as everything that is said must move the story on. Your reader will want to know what happens next. In a short story there is no room for any unnecessary words so descriptions of people and places have to be by implication. There is no room for long 'flowery' passages of description ('purple prose').

Using dialogue

Dialogue is important in the short story as it can be used to give information to the reader. (See Chapter 2 to learn how to set out dialogue.) It can also set the scene and help to create believable characters. Effective short stories often start with dialogue and this carries the reader straight into the story.

Creating believable characters

Try not to have more than four characters in your short story. Too many become confusing. Aim to give each one a distinctive way of speaking so that each can be easily recognisable. There will be no room for detailed descriptions of each so their character should be established by what they say, how they behave and how the other characters react to them.

Finding a plot

A story is written to entertain and in your story there should be conflict of some kind. It could be between a parent and child, or between two neighbours. It could be a spiritual conflict within a single character. Should the heroine have an abortion or not? The plot should be simple and there should only be one. There is no room in a short story for a sub-plot. Plots are all around you. Your own experience or someone else's could be woven into a short story or you could modernise the plot of a fairy story or a legend.

Starting the story

The start of a story is always important. The first sentence should grip the reader and carry him or her forward. Make him or her want to read on.

CHECKING YOUR WORK

When you have completed the first draft of your essay or short story, check it carefully for errors and see if it can be 'tightened' by deleting words or changing your sentence construction.

- Check your spelling.

- Check your punctuation.

- Is each paragraph indented the same amount of space?

- Have you begun your dialogue with a new paragraph?

- Have you kept to the same tense throughout? (Most essays and stories are written in the past tense.)

- In your short story have you kept to the same 'person' throughout? Is it written in the first or the third person? (See Chapter 2.)

- Have you used colloquial language?

- Before writing or typing your fair copy, look to see if you can replace any words with better ones. Make sure you haven't repeated words unnecessarily.

CHECKLIST

Writing an essay
- Keep to the point and keep the title in front of you at all times.

- Write notes in your own words. Don't copy from a book.

- Keep notes brief.
- Make a bibliography.
- Plan your work carefully.
- Structure your essay.
- Economise on words.

Plotting a short story
- Avoid unnecessary description.
- Don't have too many characters.
- Keep the plot simple.

PRACTISING WHAT YOU'VE LEARNT

1. Plan an essay using the following title:

   'Holidays abroad are a waste of time and money.' Do you agree with this statement? Give your reasons.

2. Plan the outline and write the opening of a short story. Use your own title or one of the following:

   All that Glitters

   Full Circle

   The Box

DISCUSSION POINTS

1. Why is it necessary to make notes and plan before writing an essay?

2. What purpose does dialogue serve in a short story?

3. Is it important to use different styles for different types of writing?

7
Summarising and Reporting

PRODUCING A READABLE SUMMARY

Selecting the points

Whether you have to write a summary or précis for an exam or whether you need to summarise a report for convenience, it is essential that you first thoroughly understand the meaning of the passage. Jot down the main points – using your own words. It is then a good idea to put away the original material and write the piece in your own words.

Sometimes you might be asked to summarise a piece using a certain number of words. Often the length required is a third of the original passage. Make sure you are within a word or two of the number required. Summarising is an excellent way of training yourself to write concisely. There is no room for any unnecessary words. **Adjectives** and **adverbs** should be deleted. So should any examples or illustrations. Save those for use in a longer report.

The final summary should be a competent piece of prose in your own words. It should read well and should follow all the rules you have learnt in Part 1 of this book. Study the following example:

Passage to be summarised

Napoleon and Josephine were married at a civil ceremony on 9 March 1796 after the bridegroom had kept his bride waiting for two hours. Josephine, who was thirty-two, was older than Napoleon and as her birth certificate was in Martinique, she conveniently took four years off her age. The bridegroom gallantly added a year to his so on the marriage certificate they both appeared as twenty-eight. No relations on either side were present and the Bonapartes, bitterly opposed to the marriage, pursued a vendetta against Josephine that lasted almost to the end of her life.

Napoleon soon found that he could not dominate his new wife as he could his soldiers. On their wedding night, she refused to let him remove her little dog, Fortune, from her bed where he always slept. Later her husband ruefully wrote, 'I was told that I had the choice of sleeping in another bed or sharing that one with Fortune.' The dog made his mark in history by biting the General in the leg!

The honeymoon was brief as two days after the wedding Napoleon left his new wife in Paris while he took up his post as Commander-in-Chief of the Army of Italy. From there he sent passionate love letters to her and she wrote back to him though not as frequently.

(Approximately 200 words)

Summary

Napoleon married Josephine on 9 March 1796. Both gave false ages so they were both registered as twenty-eight. The Bonapartes hated Josephine and objected to the marriage. Napoleon soon found he could not dominate his new wife as he did his soldiers. Two days after the wedding he left his wife in Paris and went to Italy as Commander-in-Chief of the army. From there he sent her frequent love letters but she did not reply very often.

(Approximately 70 words – a third of the original passage)

COMPILING A REPORT

A report, like a summary, should be concise, but examples and illustrations may be necessary in order to clarify points in the main body of the report. Unlike an essay, a report needs headings for each section and sometimes it is useful to include a brief summary of the whole report after the title page. It is important to plan the report before you start to write it. Note down all the points you hope to include and then organise them into a logical order.

Setting out the title page

The title page should contain the title of the report in the centre of the page with the name of the person who has compiled it

REPORT ON THE STATE OF ST BARNABAS
CHURCH BUILDINGS

compiled by the Churchwardens

20 March 199X

To all members of the Parochial Church Council

Fig. 4. Title page of report.

underneath. Below this is the date. This page should also show for whom the report was written. (See Figure 4.)

Using a contents table

A contents table follows the title page. This may not be necessary if the report is short. However, if it is a long report, it is useful to list the paragraph headings and the pages on which they appear.

Writing the introduction

In your introduction it is important to give the background to the report. You should explain who had asked for it, why it was written and what it is about. (See Figure 5.) Follow the Introduction with a brief summary of the Conclusions (see Figure 6).

Introduction
The Churchwardens were asked by the Parochial Church Council of St Barnabas Church to look into the state of the church buildings as it was felt that they were deteriorating. With the help of experts, they have looked in detail at the 'plant' and have decided that the time has come for a complete renovation if the buildings are to continue in use.

Fig. 5. Introduction to report.

Summary

This report shows that St Barnabas Church has fallen into a sad state of repair. The Churchwardens have consulted experts on various points and have dealt in detail with both the church itself and the adjoining church hall and facilities. As will be seen, there is a great deal that needs to be done if we are to continue to use the buildings. A number of recommendations follow the report which is to be circulated only among members of St Barnabas PCC.

Fig. 6. Summary of report.

Setting out the report

Make sure your report progresses logically from one point to the next. You have already planned it by noting all your points in the appropriate order so now write each paragraph in clear, concise prose. Use headings for each section and, unless the sections are very short, it is a good idea to start each section on a new page. This may be thought a waste of paper but it looks better and impresses the reader.

Writing the conclusion

The report should be followed by your conclusion and a list of the relevant recommendations you would like the readers to consider. Make them definite not vague. (See Figure 7.)

CHECKLIST

Summarising

- Make sure you understand the passage you are to summarise.
- Select the relevant points.
- Always write the summary in your own words.
- Write in clear, concise prose.
- Avoid unnecessary detail and examples.
- Keep to the correct number of words if told to do so.

Recommendations from the Churchwardens to the PCC

The Churchwardens have looked closely at the needs of the building and ask the PCC to take note of the following recommendations:

1. Repair the guttering on the church roof.

2. Redecorate the church hall.

3. Replace worn carpet in church hall.

4. Renovate ladies' and gents' toilet facilities.

5. Replace pews in church building with chairs and carpet the church throughout. This will cost a great deal of money. It is therefore recommended that the congregation be informed and asked to contribute to the cost. The following recommendations are also made.

   a. The collection on Sunday 23 June should be set aside for this purpose.

   b. Members of the congregation should be invited to contribute to the building fund on a regular basis.

   c. A day of prayer should be held on Saturday 22 June to pray that enough money will be given and pledged to allow us to continue using our buildings.

Fig. 7. Recommendations from report.

Reporting

- Plan your report so the points follow logically.

- Produce a title page.

- Use a contents table with page numbers.

- Write an introduction.

- Write a summary of the report.

- Use headings for each section.

- Write a conclusion including, if relevant, your recommendations.

PRACTISING WHAT YOU'VE LEARNT

1. Summarise the following passage in 50 words or less.

> Josephine continued to entertain lavishly and spent a fortune on her clothes. She changed three times a day and was said to buy six hundred dresses and a thousand pairs of gloves a year. It was hardly surprising her husband was constantly complaining about her extravagance. But on one occasion her vanity saved her life. She was late in leaving for the opera because she spent some time rearranging a shawl, a gift from Constantinople, around her shoulders.
>
> Napoleon had already left in another carriage so Josephine's carriage was some distance behind when there was a loud explosion. Fortunately Napoleon's coach had already passed the danger spot but had Josephine been following as she should have been, she would certainly have been killed as many passers-by were. It was the second attempt on Napoleon's life and the audience at the opera cheered in relief as he took his seat.

(See page 130 for suggested answer.)

2. You are a headteacher who has been asked by the governors to produce a report on the staffing position at your school. Produce a title page, an introduction and a summary of the report.

DISCUSSION POINTS

1. What is the difference between a summary and a report?

2. What purpose does a report serve?

3. Who might be asked to write a report?

8
Filling in Forms

Filling in forms is something we all have to do for all sorts of reasons. Some are straightforward. Others are more complicated. For whatever reason we have to fill in a form, it is important that it is legible and that all the information that is required is clearly set out. If it is difficult to type in the information, it is a good idea to print it so that the recipient can read it easily.

PROVIDING THE BASIC INFORMATION

Researching the market
Market researchers who send out forms to a sample of people usually require you either to tick boxes or to answer specific questions. The only personal details they might require are your age bracket, your sex, your type of living accommodation, whether you are employed and your salary bracket. These are the easiest forms to fill in although they often look daunting at first because they sometimes consist of several pages. (See example in Figure 8.)

Supplying your personal details
Apart from forms used for market research which are usually anonymous, the first page of all other forms will usually consist of your personal details (see Figure 9).

UNDERSTANDING WHAT IS REQUIRED

Dealing with the bank
Most of us, at some time, have dealings with a bank. Bank forms are usually straightforward and unless you are opening an account (see Figure 10), the two important requirements are the sort code,

Do you own your house?

Do you have a mortgage?

How many people live in your house?

Are you aged 18–25? ❏   26–40? ❏   41–60? ❏   over 60? ❏

What type of work do you do?   Professional   ❏
                                       Trade   ❏
                                       Manual   ❏
                                       Self-employed   ❏
                                       Retired   ❏

How often do you watch TV?   1–3 hours a day   ❏
                                       4–5 hours a day   ❏
                                       Over 5 hours
                                         a day   ❏

Do you take a daily newspaper?   If so which one?

Which magazines do you read regularly?

How often do you visit your local library?
                  Frequently ❏   Rarely ❏   Never ❏

Fig. 8. Example of market research form.

Name:

Address:

Telephone number: Home: Work:

Date of Birth: Nationality:

Fig. 9. Personal details on any form.

Name:

Address:

Telephone number: Home: Work:

How long have you lived at this address?

Occupation: Professional ❏   Clerical ❏   Unskilled ❏

                   Forces ❏   Self-employed ❏   Retired ❏

Name and address of present employer:

How long have you worked in your present post?

Facilities required:
Cheque guarantee card ❏   Multifunction card ❏

Overdraft: Amount: Duration: Purpose:

Amount to be paid into account monthly:

Signature: Date:

Fig. 10. Form for opening a bank account.

shown at the top right-hand corner of your cheque, and your account number, which is at the bottom of the cheque.

Opening a mortgage account
The first section of the form will be the same as in Figure 10. The following questions will be as in Figure 11.

Standing orders and direct debits
You have control over standing orders and alter the amount as necessary. A direct debit means you give the beneficiary the right to tell your bank to change the fee when there is an increase. The

Do you   – own your own home?   ❑
             – rent?   ❑
             – live with your parents?   ❑
             – live in lodgings?   ❑

What is your total annual gross (before tax) income?

Do you pay tax in the UK?

Do you pay the higher rate of tax?

Have you ever been refused credit?

If 'yes' give details.

What is your monthly expenditure?

Insurance . . .	Council tax . . .	Heating . . .	Electricity . . .
Telephone . . .	Water . . .	TV licence . . .	Car insurance . . .
Car tax . . .	Car repairs . . .	Petrol . . .	Child care . . .
Food . . .	Clothes . . .	Entertainment . . .	Other . . .

Total monthly expenditure:

Reason for mortgage:
Buying first home ❑   Second home ❑   Moving ❑

Amount of mortgage required:

Signature: Date:

Fig. 11. Form for opening a mortgage account.

sort code you will find at the top right-hand corner of your cheque.
(See Figure 12.)

Dealing with the National Health Service

You will also have to fill in a form when dealing with the National
Health Service. Fortunately the forms have recently been much
simplified. Your National Insurance Number is sometimes required

To _____ Bank

Address:

Sort code:

Please make payments from cheque account   name:
                                              number:

Please pay to   Bank name:
                       Address:
                       Sort code:

Creditor's account: name:
                       number:

The sum of: £

Amount in words:

Starting on:
and thereafter at weekly*/monthly*/quarterly*/yearly*
intervals until:
or until cancelled by me/us* in writing.

Signature: Date:

*Delete if not applicable

Fig. 12. Standing order form.

for these so make sure you keep it handy as it is often needed for other forms as well. (See Figure 13.)

Dealing with claims

Unfortunately claim forms have become a fact of life. There are few of us who, at some time, have not had to fill in one. Perhaps we've had a car accident, or been robbed, or an appliance has been damaged or broken down.

These forms will often require more than the basic details. If you have a car accident, the insurance company will need to know

Name:

Address:

Phone number:

National Insurance Number:

Name and address of previous doctor:

Please tick if you wish to register a child under five with the doctor. ❏

Fig. 13. Patient registration form.

exactly what happened. You must put into practice the rules you have learnt and write a concise account of the accident, as in the following example:

> *Details of accident*
> It was about 10.30 am on Wednesday 3 July 199X. It was raining and I had stopped at the large roundabout at the end of Send High Street. I started to drive slowly forward and realised another car was coming from the right so I stopped again. The car behind me did not stop and crashed into the back of my car, damaging the lock on the boot and smashing both rear lights. The boot cannot now be opened.

Paying by instalments

Paying for goods by instalments has become a recognised way of life as we approach the twenty-first century. 'Keeping up with the Joneses' has never been so true and we all wish for modern appliances to make our lives easier. Nowadays we do not have to pay a large amount at once. Credit cards and department charge cards are here to stay and most of us own at least one. But before one is issued, we have to fill out yet another form. As well as your personal details, you will also need to answer the questions set out in the example in Figure 14.

Name and address of bank:

Sort code: Account number:

How long have you had an account there?

Which other cards do you hold?

Mastercard ❑   Barclaycard ❑   Visa ❑
American Express ❑   Other ❑

Do you wish a card also to be issued to other members of your family?

If so, state name, address and date of birth:

Fig. 14. Application for a department charge card.

Bride's name:

Groom's name:

Date of wedding:

Bought by:

Description of gift:

Message to be put on card:

Method of payment:

Credit card number: Date of expiry:

Fig. 15. Department store wedding gift list.

Make of vehicle: Model: Engine size:
No. of doors:

Date of first registration: Registration number:

Value of vehicle: Current mileage:
Date of purchase:

Do you own the vehicle?

Is it kept in a garage?

Is it a right-hand drive?

How long have you held a driving licence?
What type is it?

Are you the main driver?

If not, please give details of other drivers:

Have you or any other mentioned drivers been involved in an
accident or suffered loss in connection with any vehicle during
the past five years?

If 'yes', please give details:

Was a claim made?

Did the accident result in a conviction?

If 'yes', please give details:

Signature: Date:

Fig. 16. Car insurance form.

Wedding gift list

Some department stores hold wedding gift lists so that guests can order appropriate gifts and have them gift wrapped and sent straight to the bride with a message. (See Figure 15.)

Taking out insurance

We all have to have insurance of some kind. Many insurances are required by law. We have to have our car and our homes insured. Fortunately these forms are not too complicated and once the first insurance has been acquired, a renewal notice only is sent in succeeding years. As well as the normal personal details, you will have to fill in details about the car (see Figure 16).

Receiving benefit

Sadly, many people have to claim benefit and to do so, it is again necessary to fill in forms. These are quite detailed but read them carefully and if you find them difficult to complete ask for help at your council or social security offices. If you are claiming housing benefit or council tax benefit, the council will want to know the following:

(a) Your personal details including date of birth and National Insurance Number. You must provide the same information for your partner if you have one.
(b) A list of children for whom you receive child benefit.
(c) Details of anyone else living in the same house.
(d) Details of your work and income including any other benefit you receive.
(e) Details of any savings you have. The council may also ask for proof of these.
(f) Details of the house in which you live.

Coping with a tax return

The tax return must be one of the most complicated forms to fill in. Fortunately the tax office provides us with a thick booklet of notes relating to specific questions. Do use this as it clarifies points that may be confusing.

Read the form through first and delete with a single line the sections that do not apply to you. As the form is comprehensive and is used for all categories from the high to the low income bracket, much of it will only apply to certain sections of the community. If you can get rid of the sections that do not relate to you, the form will not look so daunting. If you are self-employed, make sure you fill in the relevant pamphlet the Inland Revenue will send you.

If you have problems, do consult your local tax office. They are usually very helpful.

Applying for a job
Application forms will be discussed in Chapter 10.

Replying to an invitation
Wedding invitations, dinner invitations, invitations to formal banquets all require replies. On the bottom left of the invitation it will say 'RSVP to . . .'.

RSVP stands for '*Répondez, s'il vous plaît*' which is French for 'Reply please'. It *does* mean that. If you are asked to reply, do so because your host or hostess needs to know the numbers that can be expected. Courtesy suggests you should do so as soon as possible so that someone else can be invited if you are unable to accept. Remember to reply whether or not you are able to attend.

WRITING LEGIBLY

Writing legibly on a form you fill in is vital. Every form is important so make sure that the recipient of it does not have to spend time deciphering your scrawl! It is a good idea to print most of the answers. If you are required to write something, as in a car accident claim form, then remember to write legibly and concisely.

- Don't write the account of your accident straight on to the form.

- Write it out first and make sure it is clear and concise.

- Then copy it out neatly.

ASKING FOR HELP

Never be afraid to ask for help when filling in a form. Some forms can be confusing but the company will be dealing with them all the time and will be only too happy to help you. It is in their interests too. It is much better to explain something to someone than to have to request that a second form be done as the first one is incorrect.

READING THE FORMS

Do take a few minutes before you fill in a form to read it carefully. This can save you time later on. Make sure you fully understand it *before* you start to fill it in.

SIGNING YOUR NAME

Before your signature some forms put something like the following: 'I declare that to the best of my knowledge and belief the statements above are true and I have not withheld any relevant information.'

It is also likely that you may be required to have your signature witnessed. This means that you *must* let somebody *watch* you sign your name and then he or she should sign underneath to say your signature has been 'witnessed'.

CHECKLIST

- Always look through the form first and delete anything irrelevant.
- Write out any details in rough first.
- Write legibly.
- Ask for help.

PRACTISING WHAT YOU'VE LEARNT

1. You wish to make direct debit payments to the Electricity Board. Fill out the form on the opposite page.

2. Write out the details of a car accident for your insurance company.

DISCUSSION POINTS

1. Why is it necessary to read a form carefully before filling it in?

2. What purpose do forms serve?

3. Should you send a covering letter with a form?

To _____ Bank

Address:

Sort code:

Please make payments from cheque account   name:
                                            number:

Please pay to   Bank name:
                       Address:
                       Sort code:

Creditor's account: name:
                       number:

The sum of: £

Amount in words:

Starting on:
and thereafter at weekly*/monthly*/quarterly*/yearly*
intervals until:
or until cancelled by me/us* in writing.

*Delete if not applicable

9
Writing Letters

In spite of telephones, computers and the Internet, it is unlikely that letters will ever become redundant. A personal letter shows that you are thinking of someone; a business letter is a permanent record that can be produced, if necessary, as evidence at a later date. Unless it is recorded, there is no record of what was said on the telephone and a business letter can be more detailed than fax messages. Longer letters *can* be transmitted by a facsimile machine (fax) but the quality of the reproduction is not as good as the original.

WRITING A PERSONAL LETTER

Using open punctuation

Open punctuation is usually used now for letters. This means that, apart from the main body of the letter, punctuation is kept to a minimum. There are **no commas** after lines of the address and **no full stops** after abbreviations. Your address should be placed at the top right-hand corner of the page. Each line of the address should be aligned. Don't slope them. The date is set underneath it with a line space above it. Use only the figure of the date:

24 May 199X

not

24th May 199X

Leave a line under the date and on the left-hand side of the page against an imaginary margin start your letter:

Dear Mary

7 The Mount
Guildford
Surrey
GU1 9BS

3rd August 199x

Dear Joanna

Thank you so much for your last letter. I'm sorry I've taken so long to reply but life has been rather hectic here – as usual.

My mother moved into sheltered housing last week and we had to decide which of her things should be sold. Her new flat is delightful and the warden is a charming lady. It is a great relief to have her near me now that she is getting older. Although she is over eighty, she is very independent and still looks after herself.

Tomorrow my sister is coming down from Bristol and we are going out for lunch. It's ages since I've seen her as she leads such a busy life. I must close now. I have to catch up with some more correspondence before I go to bed. I'll write a longer letter next time

With best wishes

Louise

Fig. 17. Handwritten personal letter.

There is no need for a comma after 'Mary'. If the letter is handwritten, indent your paragraphs starting with the first one under 'Dear Mary'.

Your ending is up to you. The semi-formal ending is 'Yours sincerely' which is usually centred underneath the completed letter. You can also use 'With kind regards', 'With best wishes' or even 'With love'. Sign your name directly underneath the ending. See Figure 17 for an example of a handwritten personal letter.

Blocking your letter

If your letter is typed, do *not* indent. Use single spacing and leave a double space under each paragraph to separate it from the next one. This is called **blocking**. Do *not* **justify** (align) the right-hand margin.

The ending, 'Yours sincerely' or whatever you choose, is placed against the left 'margin' and you will, of course, sign your name underneath it. You may type your name underneath your signature.

WRITING A FORMAL LETTER

The same rules apply as in a personal letter but this one will, if possible, be typed and there are other rules to observe (see Figure 18). Opposite your own address, put the reference number of the company to whom you are writing – if you have one. There should be one if you have already been corresponding with the firm.

Using the name

Leave a line underneath the date and against the left-hand 'margin' write the name of the person to whom you are writing and underneath that put his or her position. Then write the address in the usual way.

If you know the name, use it. If not, start with 'Dear Sir' or 'Dear Madam'. It is better not to use 'Dear Sir or Madam' as it suggests you have not done your homework. Your letter stands a better chance of reaching the right person if it is addressed personally. Make a phone call to the company to ask the name of the Director, Sales Manager or whoever it is you wish to contact.

Ending a formal letter

The ending for a formal letter is either 'Yours sincerely' or 'Yours faithfully'. 'Yours truly', which is the same as 'Yours faithfully', is rarely used today.

'Yours sincerely' is *always* used if you have written to someone *by name*. If you have started with 'Dear Sir' or 'Dear Madam', you must end with 'Yours faithfully'. Underneath 'Yours sincerely' leave five line spaces and type in your name. If you are female, you can put your title after this in brackets:

June Brown (Mrs)

Susan Coombs (Miss)

Above your typed name sign your usual signature.

Sending an enclosure

If you have enclosed something with your letter, put 'enc' at the bottom left-hand corner of your letter and follow this with the name of the document you have enclosed. If you are asking for information, *do* remember to enclose a stamped addressed envelope (SAE). You stand a much better chance of receiving a reply if you do so.

Revising the points

- Use open punctuation.

- Block your letter.

- Do not justify your right-hand margin.

- If the letter is addressed personally, end with 'Yours sincerely'.

- If the letter begins with 'Dear Sir' or 'Dear Madam', end with 'Yours faithfully'.

- Always send an SAE if you require a reply.

PLANNING YOUR LETTER

As when writing an essay or short story, it is necessary to plan your formal letter so that the end product is the best you can produce. Think carefully about what you want to say and for whom it is intended. Note down the points you wish to make, put them in order and write your first draft avoiding any unnecessary words or 'flowery' language.

81 Queens Rd
Clevedon
Avon
BS23 9RT

16 May 199X

The Proprietor
The Angel Hotel
Mouse Lane
PRESTON
Lancs
PR1 6RA

Dear Sir

I have to spend a few days in Preston on business and I wish to book a single room at the Angel Hotel from 9 to 12 Sept 199X inclusive.

Please confirm that you have a room available and let me know your prices.

Yours faithfully

John Devine

enc SAE

Fig. 18. Formal letter.

Checking your first draft

- Don't use technical facts and figures unless you are sure your reader will understand them.

- Keep your paragraphs short.

- Don't use slang or jargon.

- Don't 'embroider' your facts. Keep them simple.

- Make sure you have a beginning, a middle and an end.

FINISHING YOUR LETTER

Using a continuation sheet

If your letter is longer than a page, use a plain sheet of paper of the same size and colour as the first. It should be plain and not headed notepaper. Under *no* circumstances write or type on the back of the first sheet.

Leave three spaces at the top of the new page. Then against the left-hand 'margin' type in '2'. Leaving a line space, write the date and after another line space put the name of the addressee. Leave three line spaces before continuing the letter.

Preparing the envelope

Set out the address on the envelope about half way down and about a third of the way across. It should be written exactly as it appears on your letter. The name of the town should always be written in capital letters. Don't forget to include the post code. (See Figure 19.)

Mr Clive Chambers
14 High Street
WORPLESDON
Surrey
GU21 5EA

Fig. 19. Addressed envelope.

WRITING DIFFERENT TYPES OF LETTERS

There are a number of different types of letters you may need to write and it is important that you find the right tone for each of them. You won't use the same tone when writing a letter of sympathy as you will when you are complaining about a faulty product or poor service. Always keep the following in mind:

- Who is to read your letter?

- Why are you writing it?

- What result do you expect from it?

Writing a letter of sympathy

This could be a personal letter to someone you know well or it could be that someone you know only slightly has been bereaved. (See Figure 20.)

- Be sympathetic but not sentimental.

- Don't patronise.

- Don't overdo flattery of the deceased.

22 Beech Grove
Grayshott
Hampshire
GU23 5RZ
14 June 199X

Dear Mrs Clarke

I was so sorry to hear of the recent death of your husband. Please accept my deepest sympathy. I only met him a few times but I remember him as a very kind, sincere man who always thought of others before himself. He will be greatly missed.

Yours sincerely
Judith Soames

Fig. 20. Handwritten letter of sympathy.

Asking for information

Whether you are asking for information about a place, a person or transport times, keep to the point. Don't include unnecessary details. List your requirements and *do* remember to enclose an SAE. (See Figure 21.)

---

12 Churchill Way
Maidstone
Kent
ME16 7OX

27 July 199X

The Curator
National Portrait Gallery
Trafalgar Square
LONDON
W1 8EA

Dear Sir

I have recently written an article about Lady Hester Stanhope for *Kent County Magazine* and the editor has asked me to supply a photograph. I believe you have one in the National Portrait Gallery and I am writing to enquire if you would permit me to use it. Please let me know the fee you would charge.

Yours faithfully

Jane Lomax

enc SAE

Fig. 21. Letter requesting a photograph.

Informing your readers

This type of letter will often be sent to a newspaper or magazine and should be addressed to the editor. Unless it is a very small

16 Prior Court
Sea Road
Bexhill-on-Sea
East Sussex
TN40 1NP

23ʳᵈ January 199x

Mrs Margaret Peters
The Editor
Bexhill Clarion
BEXHILL-ON-SEA
East Sussex
TN41 2OS

Dear Mrs Peters

I recently tripped over in the High Street and a young man came to my rescue. I was not hurt, only shaken, but I wish to thank him for his kindness as he would not give me his name.

He collected my scattered belongings, put them back in my bag and insisted on walking home with me so that he could carry my bag.

I am nearing my eightieth birthday so was very grateful for his help. His kindness has restored my faith in the younger generation.

Yours sincerely
Edith Adams

Fig. 22. Handwritten letter to a local newspaper.

publication or a local one, you can find out the name of the editor by looking in the latest edition of *The Writers' & Artists' Year Book* in your local library. If you wish to write to your local paper phone to find out the name of the editor.

Don't make your letter too long as editors have little space and a short letter is more likely to be published. (See Figure 22.)

---

30 Chertsey Road
Surbiton
Surrey
KT22 8EA

3 July 199X

The Chief Education Officer
County Hall
KINGSTON-ON-THAMES
Surrey
KT1 2RS

Dear Sir

My daughter Clare is due to start secondary school in September. We put down Cheyney High School as our first choice as it is the nearest one to our home but we were told the school was over-subscribed and she would have to go to Littlewick Manor which is ten miles away. It is not even on our bus route.

I am writing to appeal to you to act on Clare's behalf to enable her to be given a place at our nearby comprehensive school.

Yours faithfully

David Watts

Fig. 23. Letter of complaint.

Complaining about a product or a service

This is the most difficult letter to write. You must make sure you get your facts right. It is a good idea not to write the letter when you are angry. You may say things you will regret later. You should draft and redraft your letter until you are sure it conveys the facts and your feelings without being impolite or overbearing. (See Figure 23.)

Writing a letter of application for a job

This will be covered in Chapter 10.

CHECKLIST

● Use open punctuation for letters.

● If typing, block your letter.

● Use 'Yours sincerely' if the name is used.

● Use 'Yours faithfully' if starting with 'Dear Sir' or 'Dear Madam'.

● Plan your letter carefully and then draft it.

● Don't include unnecessary detail.

● Don't use slang or jargon.

● Don't patronise your reader.

● Keep to the point.

● Don't write a letter of complaint when angry.

● Don't forget to enclose an SAE if writing for information.

PRACTISING WHAT YOU'VE LEARNT

1. Write a letter to a hotel asking for details of their facilities.

2. Write a letter of sympathy to a widow you know only slightly.

3. Write a letter of complaint to a shoe firm complaining about the poor quality of some expensive shoes you have just bought.

4. Write a letter to a woman's magazine telling a short anecdote about a small child.

DISCUSSION POINTS

1. What do the terms 'open punctuation' and 'blocking' mean?

2. Why is it important to set out your letter correctly?

3. Is it better to type or hand-write a personal letter?

10
Applying for a Job

PREPARING A CURRICULUM VITAE (CV)

The preparation of a CV is becoming more and more important in the search for a job. It should be relevant and easily readable, and contain only the details that a prospective employer will need to know. He will be more interested in your achievements in your last job than in the first school you attended. Your degree is of more importance than your ten O Levels or GCSEs.

Entering your personal details

At the top of your CV you should put your full name and title, followed by your address and telephone number. Some employers will also want to know your date of birth, your marital status and your nationality so it might be worth including those. (See Figure 24.)

(Miss)	Jane Pauline Strong
	16 Ashcroft Lane
	Barking
	Essex
	RM23 8EA.
	Telephone number: (0181) 547 8192
Date of birth:	24 January 1971
Marital status:	Single
Nationality:	British

Fig. 24. CV: personal details.

Selling yourself

Your CV is a means of selling yourself and you must avoid the temptation to play down your skills and achievements. Your prospective employer will want to know whether you are suitable for the potential job for which you are applying. So make sure that you include details which highlight how suitable you would be for the post.

Writing a profile

It is a good idea to write a brief profile of yourself at the beginning. It introduces you and you should mention any relevant skill, achievements and experience. It also serves to illustrate your personal attributes. It would be useful to have two profiles – one for a specific job and one which is more general. Look at the following two examples:

Specific profile – application for a position as an assistant in a Senior Citizens' Day Centre

> A caring, adaptable individual who has worked with elderly people for several years. Has great patience and is willing to turn her hand to anything within reason.

This is relevant to the position that is being sought. The words 'caring', 'adaptable' and 'patience' are particularly appropriate.

General profile

> An articulate, forward-looking individual with great organisational ability and managerial skills. Has held a variety of jobs in middle management and is now looking for promotion. Ambitious and enthusiastic.

This profile could be used in more situations. Don't be modest when you write your profile but don't go 'over the top' and appear too good to be true.

Setting out your CV

There is no right or wrong way to set out a CV. Remember that its aim is to sell yourself so you should arrange it so that the reader can easily find what he or she wants to know. *Don't* include irrelevant detail but *do* include skills that you have acquired and your achievements.

Identifying your education

Sometimes an employer wishes to know your educational background so it is worth including that. State briefly what schools and colleges you have attended, starting with the last one and giving dates.

Presenting your qualifications

If you do not have qualifications miss out this section and concentrate on your skills and work experience however slight.

If you *are* loaded with qualifications, enter the most important ones first. It is not necessary to enter all the subjects you passed at GCSE or Advanced Level unless this is required. Follow the example below for style:

> *Qualifications*
> 1985   Associate of the London Academy of Music and Dramatic Art (Teaching diploma)
> 1984   BA (Hons) English and Theatre Studies
> 1981   3 Advanced Levels (English, History, French)
> 1979   9 Ordinary Levels (including Maths and English)

Under this section you could also include any recent training courses you have attended. Make sure they are relevant and don't include too many.

Detailing your career

Most employers will want to know what experience you have had so your work experience should be listed. Put your most recent job first and list your achievements and the skills you have developed. Go backwards and do the same with your other posts. If you have had a long career, it is not necessary to spend as much time on your first jobs.

If you are a school-leaver, you could list any holiday or Saturday jobs you have done. Again do remember to refer to the skills you have developed. (See Figure 25.)

Identifying your skills

There are a variety of skills but they fall into five main categories. Throughout our lives we are developing and sharpening them:

Career History

Company	Position held	From To
Elton's Shoe Store	Manager	June 1994–
Wyborne's Shoe Mart	Assistant Manager	Jan. 1989–May 1994
Debenham's	Sales Assistant	Jan. 1986–Dec. 1988
Harvey's	Sales Assistant	Sept. 1983–Dec. 1985

Current duties: Overseeing a staff of five.
Dealing with the public.
Ordering stock.

Skills developed: Developed communication skills.
Learnt to deal diplomatically with customers and sales representatives.
Developed tact and diplomacy when dealing with staff problems.
Developed creativity by designing window displays.

Achievements: Won an award for the best designed Christmas window 1995.
Introduced a training scheme for new young sales assistants.
Increased the sales potential of the store by customer market research.

Fig. 25. CV: career history.

- skills relating to people

- practical skills

- creative skills

- communication skills

- mathematical skills.

Including hobbies and interests

If you think it would be helpful, include a short section on your leisure time interests. This helps to give a 'rounded' picture of you and might show a prospective employer how you would fit into the firm. However, don't include too much in case your prospective employer thinks you will have no time for work!

Keep it short
Don't have your CV any longer than three pages and make it shorter if you can.

Julie Coombs
14 Seneca Road
Chertsey
Surrey
KT21 6EA
Telephone: 01932 520034

Date of Birth: 24 November 1970   Marital status: single

Profile: A conscientious, hard-working individual who enjoys working with children, has great organisational ability and is very adaptable.

Education:	Bristol University	1989–1993
	St Peter's School, Walton	1981–1989
	Hogarth Primary School, Walton	1975 – 1981

Qualifications:	PGCE (Teaching Cert.)	1993
	BA (Hons 2.1) English	1992
	3 A Levels	1989
	9 GCSEs	1987

Career history: Teacher at Prior Court, School, Weybridge 1993–present

Skills and achievements: In charge of school library for three months; developed organisational skills and patience. Helped direct two school plays and took a number of rehearsals. On pastoral committee and worked with disadvantaged children. Helped to set and organise junior examinations.

Leisure interests: Reading, listening to music, playing tennis.

Fig. 26. Example of a CV.

Application for position as:	Second in English Department	
At:	The Barn School, Borden, Hants GU35 0RZ	
Name:	Julie Coombs Title: Miss	
Address:	14 Seneca Road, Chertsey, Surrey, KT21 6EA	
Telephone:	Home: 01932 520034 Work: 01932 564033	
Date of birth:	24 November 1970	
Education:	Bristol University	1989–1993
	St Peter's School, Walton	1981–1989
	Hogarth Primary School, Walton	1975–1981
Qualifications:	PGCE (Teaching Cert.)	1993
	BA (Hons 2.1) English	1992
	3 A Levels (English, French, History)	1989
	9 GCSEs (including English and Maths)	1987
Previous posts held:	Prior Court School, Weybridge	1993–present
Position:	Teaching English at all levels Assistant librarian	

Fig. 27. Application form.

FILLING IN AN APPLICATION FORM

Some firms still issue application forms for jobs but your CV will nevertheless be useful as the forms are often very basic and there is not much room for the information. Having done your CV, you can always extract a section to include with your form.

Chapter 8 dealt with the filling in of other forms. The same rules apply to an application form. The completed form must be legible and all the information that is required must be provided. If the space is too small for your jobs or your qualifications, write in 'see attached sheet' and include the relevant sections of your CV.

Using the application form

The form will require the same personal details as any other. Following that, there may be sections for your education, qualifications and experience (see Figure 27). At the end of the form there may be a blank section in which you are asked to add anything else you think might be relevant.

WRITING A COVERING LETTER

It is always a good idea to write a covering letter to send with both a CV and an application form. It will follow the same format as the formal letter in Chapter 9. The letter can give more details and also stress your interest in the job. Don't make it too long. One side of A4 or less should be sufficient.

Handwriting or typing

It can be either handwritten or typed. If your writing is illegible, you should type, but if you can write neatly and avoid mistakes, handwriting is more personal. You should, of course, draft it out before you write the final letter. Highlight relevant points from your CV and say why you would like the position for which you are applying. (See Figure 28.)

INCLUDING REFERENCES

The names, addresses and status of your referees can be included on a separate sheet. It is not essential to include them when first applying for a job although it is sometimes useful for a prospective employer to have an immediate contact.

> Remember to check with your referees *before* submitting their names.

14 Seneca Road
Chertsey
Surrey
KT21 6EA

6 April 199X

Mr Keith Green
Headteacher
The Barn School
BORDEN
Hampshire GU35 0RZ

Dear Mr Green

I enclose an application form for the post of Second in the English Department at the Barn School.

For the past three years I have been teaching in a comprehensive school of 1,200 pupils and have had experience teaching pupils of varying abilities from 11 to 18. For the past two years I have been teaching English at A Level. During my time at Prior Court, I have been the assistant librarian and was in total charge while the librarian was on maternity leave.

I have also been involved in drama productions and have formed very good relationships with pupils and staff.

Now I feel I am ready for more responsibility and therefore I should like to apply for the vacant post. If I were appointed, I would work hard and always do my best for the school and the pupils.

Yours sincerely

Julie Coombs

Fig. 28. Covering letter.

Who to ask

Referees are usually people of standing in the community – a doctor, a vicar, a teacher.

Teachers are often asked to be referees and they are usually willing. If you have just left school, one of your teachers and your headteacher would be useful referees. But do ask them first.

You should also give your last employer. This can be difficult if he does not know you are applying for another job. It is better to let him know as the new employer will certainly get in touch. If you are a school-leaver and you have had regular Saturday or evening employment, you could ask your current boss.

CHECKLIST

- Sell yourself.

- Prepare a striking profile.

- Use only relevant material in your CV.

- List education, qualifications and jobs in reverse order – most recent first.

- Remember to include your skills and achievements but don't overdo them.

- Always write legibly.

- Remember to *ask* before offering a referee's name.

PRACTISING WHAT YOU'VE LEARNT

1. Write two personal profiles – one for a specific job and one general one.

2. Plan your CV.

3. Write a covering letter to accompany your CV. Identify the post for which you are applying.

DISCUSSION POINTS

1. What are the advantages of a CV?

2. Why should you send a covering letter?

3. Is it a good idea to include the name and addresses of referees?

Suggested Answers

CHAPTER 1

1. Putting in the full stops

John was furious. He stormed out of the house slamming the door behind him. Never again would he try to help anyone. He'd gone to Peter to offer financial aid and Peter had angrily thrown his offer back in his face. Surely he could have shown some gratitude. Now he would be late for work and he had an early appointment with an important client.

2. Using commas

The sun shone down from a brilliant blue sky, the slight breeze ruffled the long grass, the scent of roses was all around and the birds were twittering happily in the trees. Emma, who had been feeling sad, suddenly felt more cheerful. The summer had come at last, hadn't it? While she wandered down the garden path, she thought about the letter she'd received that morning.

3. Using the semi-colon, colon and dash

The team – those who were present – lined up to meet the new manager; they had had a bad season. Clive hoped Brian would improve their chances of promotion. At the moment the team was a disaster: the goalkeeper never saw the ball until it was too late, the defence players were too slow and the captain was indecisive.

4. Remembering the question mark and the exclamation mark

'I don't believe it!' she exclaimed.

'Why not?' he enquired.

Surely it could not be true. Why hadn't she been told before? It wasn't fair. Why was she always the last to hear anything? If she'd been the one going to New York, she'd probably only have heard about it after she should have left. Why had Pat been offered the chance of a lifetime? Hadn't she worked just as hard?

CHAPTER 2

1. Completing the sentences

(a) The harassed housewife rushed into the shop.
(b) Sarah ran across the road.
(c) Queen Victoria was not amused.
(d) Oxford University won the race.
(e) His cousin was very angry.
(f) He wanted to play tennis.
(g) The telephone was ringing.
(h) He worked on the computer.
(i) The castle was a ruin.
(j) The dog bit John.

2. Replacing nouns with pronouns

Sarah was working in her office. She looked out of the window and saw the window cleaner. The windows were very dirty. They needed cleaning. She asked him if he had rung the front door bell. He said he had. He asked if she wanted her windows cleaned. She said she did want them cleaned. He said the garden gate was unlocked. She was sure she had locked it. When the window cleaner rang the door bell for the second time, she heard it.

3. Correcting sentences

(a) The Government is preparing to discuss the new Divorce Bill.
(b) That class is very noisy today.
(c) Everyone had done his (her) work.
(d) The crowd was enthusiastic.

4. Adding conjunctions or relative pronouns

Although it was so cold, Judith decided to play tennis at the club. Then she discovered that her tennis racquet, **which** was very old, had a broken string. **Because** there was no time to have it mended, she knew she would not be able to play **and** she angrily threw the racquet across the room. It knocked over a china figurine **which** broke in half. She started to cry. **When** the telephone rang, she rushed to answer it **but** it was a wrong number. She picked up the broken china ornament. **If** she found some superglue, would she be able to mend it? **Before** she broke it, she had forgotten how much she liked it. **As** she had nothing better to do, she decided to go to the town to buy some glue. **While** she was shopping, she met Dave **who** invited her to a party that evening. She was thrilled **as** she had been feeling very depressed.

5. Adding phrases

(a) **Flinging open the door,** he hurtled into the room.
(b) He broke his leg **falling off his horse.**
(c) Mr Samson, **a tall, elegant man,** walked on to the stage.
(d) **Climbing into bed,** she thought about the events of the day.
(e) **Bouncing her ball,** the child giggled.

6. Indirect speech

John asked Susan if she would go to the dance. Susan replied that she couldn't because she was going to a wedding.

7. Play

Ruth: I've got so much to do.
Brian: The wedding's not for ages.
Ruth: But there's food to order, the wedding cake to make and the dresses to buy. (Starts to clear table)
Brian: (Goes to door) I have to go to the office today. I'll be back for dinner.
Ruth: Wait. I want you to do some shopping for me. I've got a list somewhere.

CHAPTER 3

1. Plurals

ladies, companies, monkeys, tomatoes, boas, princesses, dances

2. Verbs

dining, living, hitting, hopping, skipping, writing, mating, mining

3. Adverbs

happily, joyfully, kindly, angrily, wonderfully, clearly, quickly, carelessly

4. Completing the passage

There were no ships on the **sea** that morning. She could **see** the white foam as the waves crashed on the shore. She would **know** when **their** car arrived as it would drive **through** the gate. Idly, she **threw** a stone into the **sea.** The **boughs** of the trees on the cliff **were** swaying in the wind. It was **too** cold **to** sit still. Kicking off her sandals, she noticed she had **two** holes in her socks. She had intended to **wear** her new ones. Her hair ribbon had also come undone and crossly she tied it in a **bow** and stood up, holding her shoes. **Now** she could **hear** the car.

5. Initials

n.	noun
v.t.	verb transitive
v.i.	verb intransitive
a.	adjective
adv.	adverb

6. Synonyms

It was a **sunny** day so the children decided to have a picnic. They **sauntered** along the cliff path and **clambered** down to the beach. The waves crashed on the shore as they ate their **delicious** lunch.

CHAPTER 4

1. Apostrophes

Carefully he picked up John's bundle. It wasn't very heavy. He glanced warily at the cave's entrance. It was very dark. The picnic baskets still lay where they'd been thrown. He stepped into the cave and almost fell over a pile of little rubber tubes that looked like mice's tails. Inside there was a boulder of rock. Its smooth surface glistened like gold. David's hands shook. He wished he'd stayed with his brothers. His parents' quarrel had upset him and that was why he'd run away. In a week's time they were going on holiday. He wished now that he'd stayed at home as he'd been told.

2. Abbreviations

The foll. doc. from Mrs Barker gives info. about the lectures to be given by Prof. Peter Coombs in Sept. and Oct. in St Margaret's Church Hall. The Hall is in Church Rd and is situated near the station. Prof. Peter Coombs will be accompanied by Dr Martin.

CHAPTER 5

1. Corrections

(a) The school is hoping to raise enough money to build a new drama studio.

(b) He gave packages to both John and me.

(c) I and June are going out.

(d) The cat licked its whiskers while the dogs ate their dinner.

(e) Her work was excellent.

(f) He hasn't got a coat.
    He's got no coat.

(g) She could have gone to London.

CHAPTER 7

1. Summary

Josephine spent a fortune on her clothes and Napoleon complained about her extravagance. But on one occasion her vanity saved her life. Because she had spent extra time arranging a new shawl around her shoulders, her carriage left late and she consequently missed the bomb that killed several bystanders. (49 words)

Glossary

Acronym. A word formed from the initial letters of other words.

Adjective. A word that describes a noun.

Adverb. A word that qualifies a verb, an adjective or another adverb.

Bibliography. A list of books that have been used.

Clause, dependent. A group of words containing a verb that depends on the main clause. They cannot stand alone.

Clause, main. A group of words that contain both a subject and a verb and make sense by themselves.

Conjunction. A word that links two clauses together.

CV (Curriculum Vitae). A resumé of one's education, qualifications and jobs held.

Gerund. A present participle used as a noun.

Inverted commas. Speech marks: put around speech and quotations.

Jargon. Words or expressions used by a particular group of people.

Justify. Adjust margins so they are level.

Metaphor. An implied comparison of two things.

Noun, abstract. A word that denotes a quality or state.

Noun, collective. A singular word which refers to a group of people or things.

Noun, common. The name of a thing.

Noun, proper. The name of a person or place. It always begins with a capital letter.

Object. A **noun** or **pronoun** that follows the **verb** and is related to the **subject**.

Paragraph. A group of sentences dealing with the same topic.

Personify. Giving an inanimate object human characteristics.

Phrase. A group of words not necessarily containing a verb or making sense on its own.

Plagiarism. Using someone else's work as your own.

Preposition. A word that governs a noun or pronoun.

Pronoun, interrogative. A pronoun that is used at the start of a question.

Pronoun, personal. A word that takes the place of a noun.

Pronoun, relative. This has a similar role to a **conjunction**. It joins **clauses** together but is closely linked to a **noun**.

Prose. Written or spoken language without regular rhythm or rhyme.

Referee. Someone who is asked to give a reference to an employer.

Simile. A comparison of two things using 'like' or 'as'.

Subject. The **noun** or **pronoun** on which the rest of the **clause** depends.

Summary. A shortened version of a longer piece of writing.

Synonym. A word that can be used to replace another.

Tautology. A statement that is repeated in a different way in the same sentence.

Thesaurus. A book which will give a selection of synonyms.

Topic sentence. The main sentence in a paragraph. This is elaborated in the rest of the paragraph.

Verb, intransitive. A **verb** that is *not* followed by an **object**.

Verb, transitive. A **verb** that *is* followed by an **object**.

Further Reading

The King's English, Fowler, Oxford.

Mastering Business English: How to improve your business communication skills, Michael Bennie (How To Books, 3rd edition 1996).

Roget's Thesaurus, Longman.

Write Right, Jan Venolia, David St John Publisher.

Writing an Essay: How to improve your performance for coursework and examinations, Brendan Hennessy (How To Books, 4th edition 1997).

Writing a Report, John Bowden (How To Books, 4th edition 1997).

Index

Abbreviations, 57–9, 66
Acronyms, 59
Active voice, 73
Adjectives, 33–4
Adverbs, 34
Apostrophes, 55–7, 66
Application forms, 121–2

Bibliography, 79

Capital letters, 24
Clauses:
  dependent, 30–1, 75–6
  main, 29–31, 75–6
Clichés, 70
Colons, 17
Commas, 13–17
Comparisons, 67–8
Conjunctions, 14, 29–31
Contractions, 58–9, 66
Covering letter, 122–3
CV, 116–120

Dashes, 18
Dictionary, 51–2
Direct speech, 16, 38–41

Essay writing, 78–82
Exclamation marks, 18–19

Forms, 92–103
Full stops, 11, 13, 61

Gerunds, 23
Grammar, 21–42

Indirect speech, 41
Infinitives, 22–3
Inverted commas, 38–41

Jargon, 69
Job applications, 116–124

Letter writing, 104–114

Metaphors, 71

Nouns, 21, 64–5
  abstract, 28
  collective, 27
  common, 21, 24
  proper, 24

Object, 52, 62–4

Paragraphing, 35–8
Participles, 23
Passive voice, 73
Personification, 71–2
Phrases, 33
Plagiarism, 79
Play form, 41–2
Plurals, 46–8
Prepositions, 34–5
Pronouns:
  interrogative, 32

personal, 24–5, 62–4, 66
possessive, 56
relative, 31
Prose, 72
Punctuation, 11–19, 61–2

Question marks, 18, 32
Quotation marks, 40–1

References, 122, 124
Reports, 87–91

Semi-colons, 16–17, 61–2
Sentences, 11–19, 61–2, 67, 75–6
Similes, 70–1
Spelling, 46–53, 64–5

Story writing, 83–4
Style, 72–6
Subject, 15, 24–5, 62
Summary, 86–7
Synonyms, 52–3

Tautology, 66–7
Thesaurus, 52–3
Topic sentences, 36–7

Verbs, 21–4, 62–5
finite, 22
non-finite, 22
intransitive, 52
transitive, 52
Vocabulary, 53

MAKING A WEDDING SPEECH
How to prepare and present a memorable speech

John Bowden

At thousands of weddings each year, many people are called on to 'say a few words'. But what do you say? How do you find the right words which will go down really well with the assembled company? Written by an experienced and qualified public speaker, this entertaining book shows you how to put together a simple but effective speech well suited to the particular occasion. Whether you are the best man, bridegroom, father of the bride or other participant, it will guide you every step from great opening lines to apt quotations, anecdotes, tips on using humour, and even contains 50 short model speeches you can use or adapt to any occasion.

166pp. 1 85703 347 7. 3rd edition.

SELLING YOUR HOUSE
How to manage your agent, find the best buyer and complete the sale

Adam Walker

Almost everyone who has ever sold a house has a horror story to tell about the experience. This book explains in clear, jargon free terms, every stage of the sales process and gives an insider's view on how to avoid all the most common pitfalls. You will learn how to choose the right estate agent, how to set the optimum price for your property and negotiate an offer, and how to reduce the chances of a sale falling through. During his 15 years as a management consultant specialising in the residential property market, Adam Walker has advised more than 350 estage agency firms and trained more than 10,000 of their staff.

144pp. illus. 1 85703 287 X.